THE GOLDEN GUIDE TO

GUNS

by LARRY KOLLER

This title originally published
in the Golden Guide series.

GOLDEN PRESS • NEW YORK
Western Publishing Company, Inc.
Racine, Wisconsin

Illustrations by **G. DON RAY**

PHOTO CREDITS:

Bill Browning, Montana Chamber of Commerce:
pages 45 (lower right), 46, 49 (top right), 57 (bottom),
112 (top), 113, 117, 121 (top), 160.
Robert Elman: page 32
Larry Koller: Cover Ektachrome, pages 49 (left
center), 84 (left center), 117, 124, 125, 154, 155, 157.
Leonard Lee Rue III: pages 33 (left center,
upper left), 37 (top), 49 (right center), 52-53, 81 (top),
84 (top left and right, right center, bottom),
88 (bottom), 96 (bottom).
Fred Space: pages 45 (lower left), 56 (bottom).
West Point Museum: pages 6, 7.
Graham Wilson: pages 45 (center), 57 (top right).

The editors wish especially to thank the following manufacturers
for their help in the preparation of this book: Colt's Patent Firearms, Remington Arms Company, Savage Arms Company, Smith
& Wesson, Winchester Repeating Arms Company.

CONTENTS

HISTORY OF AMERICAN

• The power of a gun to deliver a lethal blow accurately and at long range has fascinated men for nearly 700 years. The invention of gunpowder in 13th-century Europe made the gun possible—and inevitable. And once it had appeared, gunsmiths and armorers inevitably applied skill and ingenuity to refining it and increasing the efficiency with which it performed its task.

Today the explosive force of gunpowder has been effectively channeled and the gun is an instrument of great precision. It is a far cry from its crude, eccentric ancestors, and yet it is recognizably their true descendant. Any man who raises a gun to his shoulder, sights down the barrel, and squeezes the trigger inherits—and perpetuates—something from the vivid past.

More than that, he contributes something of himself to the magic of the gun. For it is only his agent. It will respond swiftly and ably only to the extent that it is handled with resolution and respect. For good or ill, it

GUNS

voices and executes the intentions of the gunner. Daniel Boone, John Wilkes Booth, Billy the Kid, and Sergeant York—all were men with guns in their hands.

Much of the gun's history is American. Guns have figured prominently in many of the nation's early days. They were present in the earliest seacoast settlements, helped secure the independence of a new nation, opened the West, and sang of triumph and tragedy in wars at home and abroad. Today, as the result of a constitutionally guaranteed freedom to keep and bear arms, guns are the companions of more than 15 million hunters, sportsmen, marksmen, and collectors.

The first truly American gun was the Kentucky rifle. Long, slim, and as accurate as it was beautiful, it appeared in the 1720's, developed slowly for half a century, and achieved perfection of form and function in time to help win the American Revolution.

The guns that preceded it were European imports. Explorers of the late 1500's and early 1600's came ashore with matchlock muskets, unwieldy, uncertain, and unlovely weapons that smoked and roared impressively, but were useless if the slow-burning twist of hemp—the match—that ignited the powder charge was ever extinguished. In time, other locks—firing mechanisms—journeyed to the New World, chief among them the flintlock, for more than 100 years the world's principal firearm. Generally, it fired a single, large-caliber ball that was loaded at the muzzle and tamped into

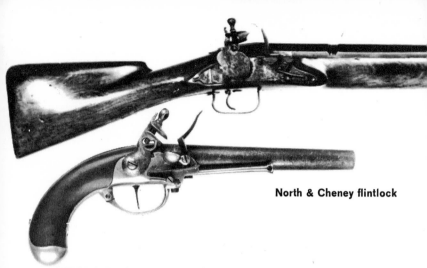

North & Cheney flintlock

place—"seated"—with a ramrod. Flint struck steel—hammer against "frizzen"—with a pull of the trigger and the resulting sparks ignited the charge in a priming pan. The flame spurted through a "touch hole" drilled in the side of the barrel and exploded the main charge. Smoothbore, .78-caliber flintlock muskets, such as the British Redcoat's "Brown Bess" or the American revolutionary's French Charleville, could be loaded and fired four times a minute by an expert and were accurate up to 100 yards. This was sufficient range for fusillades against massed infantry, which were a standard military tactic of the time.

The .45-caliber Kentucky was a sharpshooter's weapon, better adapted than the musket to the requirements of the frontiersman whose targets—animal or human—lurked in a wooded wilderness. It was the design on which future models would be built. Its action was similar to the musket's, except that the spiral grooves cut in the barrel—rifling—imparted spin to the ball, thus giving it greater speed and accuracy. A good rifleman could drop a deer at 100 yards, a redskin at 200. (The

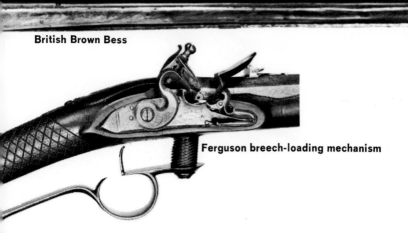

British Brown Bess

Ferguson breech-loading mechanism

brisk trade with the Indians—guns for furs and allegiance—never involved the treasured Kentucky, however. Trade guns were smoothbore flintlocks, usually short-barreled carbines whose stocks were brightly decorated with brass studs, but whose quality was less than the best.)

The vital importance of the gun on the advancing frontier of the new nation was reflected in the persistent efforts to improve its rate of fire, reliability of discharge, striking power, and range. Loading at the breech to eliminate the labor of muzzle-loading was a first step. Major Patrick Ferguson, a capable British officer, developed an ingenious breechloader during the Revolution, but it did not find favor with the military and the idea died with him at the Battle of King's Mountain in 1780. In 1811, an American inventor, Captain John Hall, designed a partially successful breech-loading flintlock, but flame invariably spurted from the loose joints of the chamber. Halls were used in the Mexican War and a few even in the Civil War, but were too hazardous ever to be popular.

7

Ornate stock of Kentucky rifle

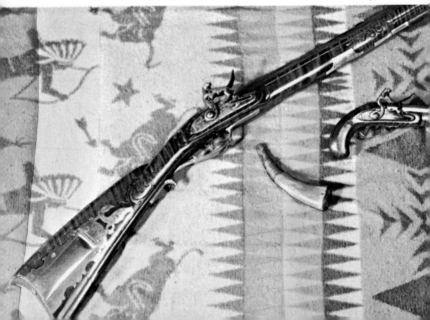

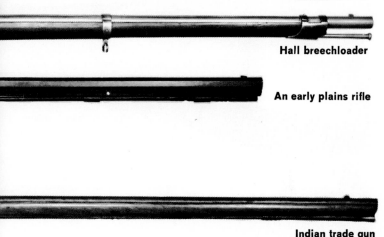

Hall breechloader

An early plains rifle

Indian trade gun

HISTORY OF AMERICAN GUNS

Techniques and machinery were needed to produce precision parts with closer tolerances. Eli Whitney, the inventor of the cotton gin, was among the first to develop interchangeable (although substantially hand-made) parts and assembly line production. Hall himself was a resourceful inventor and Eliphalet Remington, who started the first full-scale gun factory in 1816, installed Hall's precision equipment when he expanded his business in 1828. But it was not until 1848 that Christian Sharps, who had worked at the Harpers Ferry arsenal under Captain Hall, finally developed a satisfactory breechloader.

The Sharps also used a one-piece cartridge which helped greatly to overcome the powder flare that plagued the Hall. Self-contained cartridges had be-

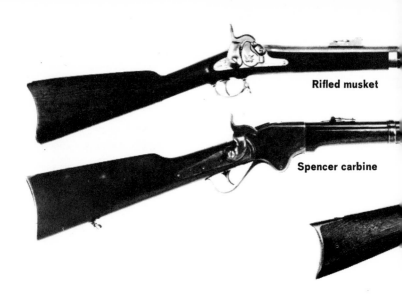

Rifled musket

Spencer carbine

come feasible in the 1820's with the introduction of percussion ignition. A metal cap filled with an explosive chemical compound was seated on the tip of a hollow tube—the cone, or nipple—that led to the main powder charge. The percussion of hammer on cap sent a jet of flame through the cone to ignite the powder. Once and for all, this eliminated the disconcerting misfires caused by faulty ignition.

The first important gun adapted for percussion ignition was the Hawken brothers' "plains rifle." This was a Kentucky type with a shorter barrel and bigger bore. It could take a fearsome load and was used by mountain men and trappers against grizzlies, buffalo, and other heavy game encountered west of the Mississippi.

Maximum firepower, however, awaited repeating weapons. Sam Colt's revolving rifles and pistols appeared first, in the famous Paterson models of 1836.

10

.44-caliber Henry

Sharps carbine

Then Sharps produced his breechloader. It was a single-shot weapon, but its self-contained cartridge was the essential element that would make true repeaters possible.

The big Sharps survived through the 1800's. Handling big-bore metallic cartridges that could kill at a quarter-mile range, it was the prime single-shot arm of the buffalo hunter and Indian sniper through the rugged period of hide-hunting and the Plains Wars. Its place in history is firm with the rifleman who respects great power and deadly accuracy at long range.

The Army, lagging somewhat behind firearms developments elsewhere, used a .54-caliber, single-shot rifled musket as its principal Civil War weapon. Two fine repeaters were available, but saw only limited service: the seven-shot, .52-caliber Spencer and the 16-shot, .44-caliber Henry. Both used the efficient new

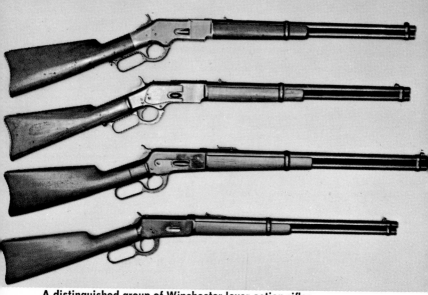

A distinguished group of Winchester lever-action rifles.
From top to bottom: Models 1866, 1873, 1886, and 1894. The last,
designed by John Browning, is still a popular deer rifle.

HISTORY OF AMERICAN GUNS

rim-fire metallic cartridge introduced by Horace Smith and Daniel Wesson in 1858. The Spencer, although known to the Confederates as "that damned Yankee rifle that can be loaded on Sunday and fired all week," was never a success after the war. The lesser-known Henry, however, became the most popular repeater in the arsenal of the western range rider, Indian fighter, and scout.

In a few years, it grew into the Winchester Model 1866, which remained the major arm of hunters, scouts, and cattlemen for almost twenty years. The Model 1873, chambered for a .44-40 bullet, was rejected by the military for whom it was designed, but 720,610 of these famous guns were sold before it was discontinued in 1924. The Winchesters, together with the distinguished series of Colt handguns that began in 1836

and culminated in the Peacemaker, were unsurpassed in popularity. When in 1878 the Peacemaker was chambered for the same .44-40 cartridge used in the Winchester '73, they provided the plainsman with two weapons for one load and became, indeed, "the guns that won the West."

The handgun, the sidearm of the military and personal combat weapon of the frontiersman, gradually incorporated the advances made in long arms. From their first appearance, the Colt revolvers led the field. The quality and volume of his output earned Sam Colt an honored position in the history of firearms. His output ranged from the .44 Walker Colt, which weighed over four pounds, through the Dragoon series, to a .31-caliber pocket pistol, introduced in 1849, which was one of his most popular and long-lasting models. His

13

major rivals were Remington's big .36 and .44 calibers, which had a solid frame bridging the cylinder that for a while made them stronger than the Colts and also provided a sighting groove.

Smith and Wesson, who become partners in 1856, made the transition from percussion caps to metallic cartridges in handguns, as they had with long arms. A year later, they acquired a Rollin White patent for boring cylinders clean through, thus permitting the swift insertion of cartridges from the rear of the cylinder. Incidentally, White originally offered the patent to Colt. Not thinking in terms of metallic cartridges, Sam made the mistake of turning it down. Smith and Wesson thereby obtained a virtual monopoly on cartridge revolvers. Just as their big .44-caliber Number 3, or American, was beginning to hit the market in 1869, however, the White patent expired and competitors could move into the field.

The military, which had offered considerable resistance to advancements in rifles, proved much more receptive to handgun improvements. The first official pistol—a copy of the French model of 1777—was made by North & Cheney in 1799. After that the designs were all American. Although it thoroughly tested all makes of revolvers, the Army, like the civilian frontiersmen, preferred the Colts. Military purchases of the Walker Colt, the Dragoon series, the Army Model 1860, and the Peacemaker contributed to the support of side-arm development.

Perhaps the most influential gun designer this country has produced was John Moses Browning who, from the issue of his first patent in 1879, designed a cascade of guns for Winchester, Remington, and Colt. He and

14

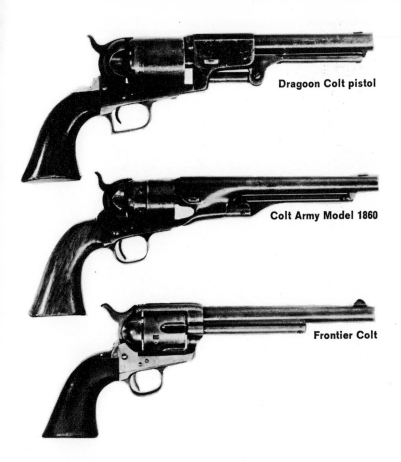

Dragoon Colt pistol

Colt Army Model 1860

Frontier Colt

his brother later formed their own arms company. Browning's achievements in the autoloading field are unparalleled and include the famous Government Model 1911 Colt automatic pistol—still the official U.S. Army sidearm.

Under the spur of necessity, American ingenuity has created a great array of firearms in every era of its history. The current high points of gun evolution are described and pictured on the pages that follow. The fascination for straight shooting still exists.

THE RIFLE
PART 2

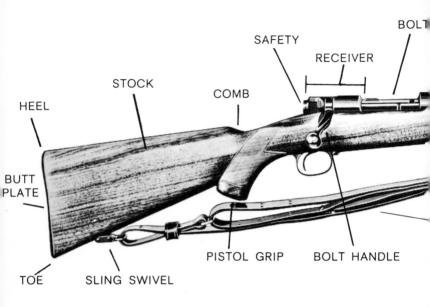

HEEL

STOCK

COMB

SAFETY

RECEIVER

BOLT

BUTT
PLATE

TOE

SLING SWIVEL

PISTOL GRIP

BOLT HANDLE

• The distinguishing characteristic of the rifle is the series of shallow, spiral grooves cut into the inner surface of its barrel. These channels—rifling—impart spin to the bullet as it is forced through the barrel by the explosion of the powder charge, thus assuring a steadier, more accurate bullet flight over a greater range than would be possible if the bore were smooth.

Rifling was known as early as the 16th century in Germany, but was first applied successfully in the Kentucky rifle and did not reach peak efficiency until the development of metallic ammunition. For while the Kentucky was more accurate than the smoothbore muskets of its time, it fired a round ball whose poor ballistic qualities shortened its range. The streamlined conical bullet used today is far better able to buck wind and maintain its velocity over long ranges.

To perform properly a rifle must be loaded with a bullet slightly larger in diameter than the uncut surfaces of the bore. This discrepancy permits the rifling

18

Preceding pages: Weatherby Mark V

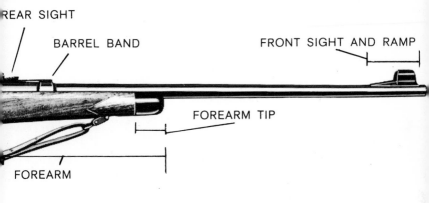

REAR SIGHT

BARREL BAND

FRONT SIGHT AND RAMP

FOREARM TIP

FOREARM

SLING

WHAT MAKES A RIFLE

to grip the bullet firmly and apply the twist that will stabilize it in flight. The usual rifle has eight grooves, but there may be as few as two or as many as 16. Generally, the more grooves the greater the stability of the bullet.

Grooves also are cut at varying "rates of pitch" which govern the speed of a bullet's rotation. Low-velocity rifles, for instance, have a "slow" pitch, perhaps one complete turn in 26 inches, whereas a high-velocity rifle, such as a Model 70 Winchester or a .257 Weatherby Magnum, will have one turn every 10 inches.

Different rates of pitch require different types of bullets. Lead or lead-alloy bullets are good only in low-velocity rifles. High-speed rifling would strip shreds of metal from the soft lead, thereby distorting the bullet's ballistic qualities, as well as fouling the grooves. High-velocity bullets are jacketed with copper alloy which is hard enough to withstand stripping and to protect the lead core from melting.

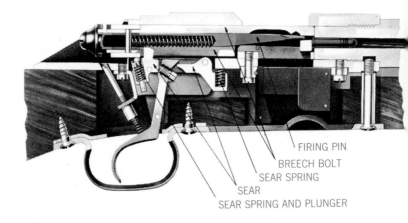

FIRING PIN
BREECH BOLT
SEAR SPRING
SEAR
SEAR SPRING AND PLUNGER

BOLT: Winchester Model 52 shown in closed and locked position with Long Rifle cartridge in chamber, firing pin at full cock. Rifle is ready for firing. Cutaway shows adjustable trigger-pull

HOW RIFLE ACTIONS WORK

• There are four principal rifle actions. Choosing among them is most often based on the shooting conditions the hunter will encounter and the kind of game he is hunting. Frequently, however, the shooter's personality can be a factor and should be taken into consideration.

BOLT ACTION: This is the strongest, heaviest type, and is best for long-range accuracy and precise shooting without exceptionally fast repeat-fire. It is the only action strong enough to take such powerful cartridges

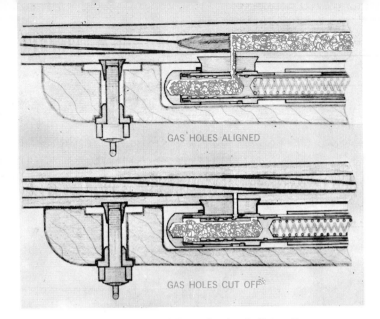

GAS HOLES ALIGNED

GAS HOLES CUT OFF

AUTOMATIC: Winchester Model 100 showing bullet as it passes bore port, releasing gas into operating cylinder. Pressure forces piston to close, cutting off proper amount of gas to work action

as the Winchester .458 for use against dangerous game. Usually stocked to give the easiest, most comfortable shooting with a telescopic sight, it holds four to five shots in large calibers, six to eight in smaller ones. This is a good action for the nervous hunter. The manual activity required to ready it for each shot tends to steady the shooter and prevents him from firing too rapidly.

LEVER ACTION: Originally, this rifle was well suited for carrying on horseback because of its flat, compact shape. The older designs proved too lightly constructed for heavy loads, but today's lever-actions are built for such high-pressure cartridges as Winchester's .243, .308, and .358. Small-calibers, like the .22, can hold up to 15 shots, or more.

PUMP (OR SLIDE) ACTION: Pumps are generally lightweight, easy to handle, and quick to get on target, but they are usually longer barreled and less maneuverable in brush country than lever-actions. An exception is the new Remington Model 760 C, with its barrel

LEVER: Marlin Model 336 with the action fully opened. Empty cartridge has just been ejected and bolt is now started forward, forcing loaded cartridge into chamber

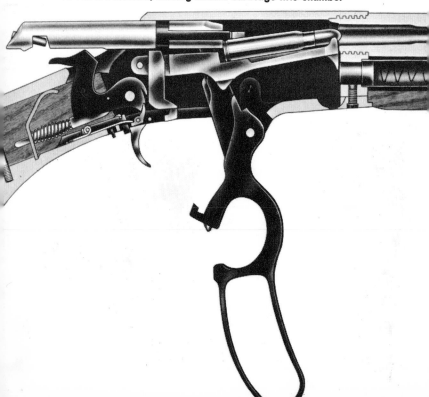

length of 18½ inches. An exceptional shooter can operate a pump as fast as a semi-automatic rifle.

AUTOLOADER: This fires faster than any other action and is preferred by some hunters in rapid-fire shooting for such game as whitetail deer. Autos are heavier than pumps or levers, and because of their more complex parts are liable to mechanical difficulties—fouling, jamming, etc. Because of their rapid-firing ability, they should be used by calm, disciplined hunters who are not inclined to spray the landscape with bullets.

PUMP: Pulling back on the slide handle of a pump action causes the used cartridge to be ejected through the port. Forward movement chambers the fresh cartridge and locks the breech block

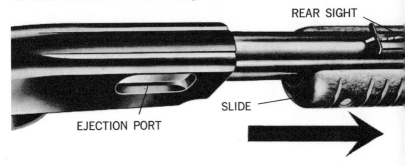

REAR SIGHT

SLIDE

EJECTION PORT

CALIBERS

• Caliber is the diameter of a rifle bore designated in thousandths of an inch. It is generally measured between opposite grooves, but in some cases, from land to land (the bore surface remaining after the grooves have been cut). Bullet diameters, as they relate to a rifle's caliber, are groove-to-groove measurements.

Rifles and the cartridges that fit them must be of the same caliber. There is some confusion in designations because manufacturers try to give their cartridges an identity that will always be associated with the company. This results in such various names as the .30-30 Winchester, .30 Remington, .300 Savage, and .300 Weatherby Magnum. All of these rifles shoot the same diameter of bullet. The variation is simply in bullet weight and shape. The .308 Winchester, measured from groove to groove, and the old .30 Winchester, which used the land diameter, shoot a bullet of exactly the same diameter. The .008 is the difference between the measurements from land to land, and from one .004-inch groove to its opposite. In the .25 series of cartridges, the .25-35 and .250 Savage use the land-to-land designation, while the more modern .257 Roberts and .257 Weatherby Magnum employ the groove method. Most rifles may be chambered for different calibers of cartridge, but they will then fire only that cartridge.

AMMUNITION

• A cartridge is a compact unit, or load, composed of primer, powder charge, and bullet. The bullet is the projectile and is propelled by the interacting forces of primer and powder. As no rifle suits all situations and no cartridge fits every rifle, no bullet is suitable for all shooting. Shape and construction dictate usage. For example, heavy, compact bullets, capable of achieving high velocities and penetrating tough hides, are needed for big game, but will drill through smaller animals. If small edible game is the quarry, low-velocity loads are best; the tremendous expansion of high-velocity bullets destroys meat. More potent loads—blunt-nosed and metal-jacketed types—are saved for dangerous game.

These are sporting bullets, so-called because they kill quickly by expanding larger than their original caliber as they enter the target, thereby providing greater shocking power. This permits a well-placed shot to drop the animal rather than let it escape, wounded, to die later in agony.

Military bullets, in order to comply with the rules of international warfare, are equipped with a full-metal case (no lead tip exposed), so that no expansion occurs and an unnecessarily painful wound is less likely to be inflicted.

25

BULLETS

Sporting bullets have a core of lead or lead alloy over which a jacket of copper-zinc alloy may or may not be placed, according to the demands of game and rifle. By varying the thickness and design of this jacket metal, ammunition manufacturers can control the degree of bullet expansion. Three degrees exist in sporting loads: soft point, hollow point, and expanding.

The effectiveness of a bullet is measured by its striking force, which is dependent on a combination of variables: expansion, weight and shape, and the velocity maintained over a required distance. Ideally, bullets would perform best if they were all of moderate weight and equipped with sharply pointed tips, since they would meet less air resistance. However, bullet conformations as to weight and shape are limited by the

26

construction of each rifle and the type of action associated with given calibers. No matter how constructed, two forces—gravity and air—impede the bullet's progress and affect its trajectory. This simultaneous resistance causes the bullet to lose momentum immediately as it is ejected from the rifle muzzle, and to lose speed gradually over the flight path. As the bullet slows, gravity is able to exert greater control over it, producing a gently sloping downward curve. Variations in weight, shape, and velocity can increase or decrease the length of this curve, and the shooter, if he is to be accurate, must be able to calculate for the curve when aiming. A study of loads and of bullet velocities at various ranges is necessary. Manufacturers' tables provide much of this information.

SMALL-BORE RIFLES

• No other class of firearm is made in such a variety of actions and designs as the .22 rim-fire rifle. Most models fire all three sizes of .22-caliber rim-fire cartridges—Short, Long, and Long Rifle. The Long Rifle—in standard or high-speed loading—is the favorite cartridge of the target rifleman. The high-speed, hollow-point, Long Rifle cartridge is perfect for squirrel, rabbit, or other small pests. In addition to the wide range of shooting experiences possible with .22 rifles and .22-rifle loads, they are relatively inexpensive to shoot, produce little report or recoil, and are accurate enough to permit shooters to develop a high degree of skill. While the .22 doesn't pack the punch of larger calibers, it is a basic tool for every rifleman. For the plinker of tin cans, it peppers the target and offers a great amount of shooting at low cost. For serious target and small-game riflemen, shooting in confined quarters, the disintegrating bullet load of the .22 provides maximum protection from ricochet and lead spatter.

AUTOLOADERS are without question the most popular repeating models in the .22 family. They are particular favorites among plinkers, since they function with all three cartridge sizes. In fact, these models, as well as pump-action models, are generally regarded as the real "fun guns" which normally are not selected for serious target or small-game shooting. The basic ob-

SMALL-BORE RIFLES

jection to the autoloader made by most skilled rifle-men is that trigger-pull tends to be rough and does not permit clean let-off, that is, a smooth, even movement without "play" or "creep." Since trigger control is not quite positive, the shooter's chances for accuracy are directly affected. This does not mean that accuracy is impossible with the autoloader; some of these models can be remarkably sharp. One Marlin 98, fitted with cheek-piece stock and 20X scope (which magnifies the target 20 times), gave 1⅛-inch groups at 100 yards. Most autoloaders have large-capacity tubular magazines (some hold as many as 30 Short cartridges), but this is not always true. Originally, cartridges were fed into the chamber horizontally from a tube in the butt, a method used in the old Winchester Model 63, Marlin Models 98 and 99, Remington Model 66 with a nylon stock, and Mossberg Model 151. Although reliable, this method of feed limits the magazine capacity to 15, or as few as 10 Long Rifle cartridges. The under-barrel tubular magazine, feeding up into the chamber on an

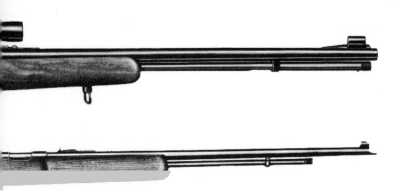

Basic equipment for riflemen, the .22-caliber rifle is made in the widest range of actions and designs. Shown here, Mossberg Model 346-K with 4X scope sight (top) and Savage Model 5 De Luxe. Both feature Monte Carlo stocks, have tubular magazines

angle, will carry from 15 to 18. Remington Models 550 and 552, Stevens Model 87, Savage Model 6, Marlin Model 99, and High Standard Pump Sport-King and Automatic Sport-King also feed cartridges in this way.

BOLT-ACTION MODELS: In small-game and serious target shooting, bolt-action models are preferred. They permit smooth trigger-pull and come equipped with stocks designed for scope shooting. In addition, the bolt-action closure gives better breech lock-up to rim-fire cartridges. All of these factors assure the shooter of greater accuracy. Almost any model will produce two-inch groups at 100 yards. Models are manufactured in 20-odd designs and a wide choice of weights ranging from five to eight pounds. A serious shooter usually selects a heavier model because of its better holding (or gripping) qualities, although the fact that the shooter can grip his rifle more firmly does not necessarily insure greater accuracy. The Ruger Model 10/22, Remington 511A, Marlin 80, Savage 5, all clip-loaded (with .22 Long Rifle only) are the preferred rifles in this

31

class. The clip, or box, magazine offers hunters in the field the convenience of converting from regular to hollow-point or other loads by simply inserting the proper magazine. In tubular magazine models (the Marlin Model 81-DL and Savage 5 are good ones), the tube must be cleared before the desired cartridges can be inserted (one by one).

SLIDE AND LEVER ACTIONS: Both of these perform equally well and make good all-around choices for plinkers and small-game hunters. Slide, or pump, actions have tubular magazines, capable of using all three .22 loads. They're dependable when the action is clean, but lack the accuracy of bolt-action models because they do not lock up as tightly as the bolts. Once highly popular, they are now losing their promi-

Plinking—informal target practice with tin cans, clay birds, etc.—can be combined with small-game hunting to develop skill in prone, sitting, and standing positions. The shooter below uses a scoped bolt action. The open-sighted rifles on facing page are (from top) a slide action, lever action, and autoloader.

Porcupine: literally "spiny-pig"

Snowshoe rabbit, or varying hare

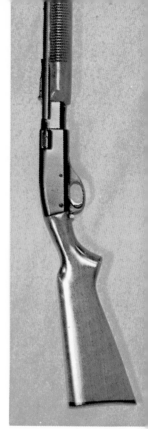

Remington Model 572A

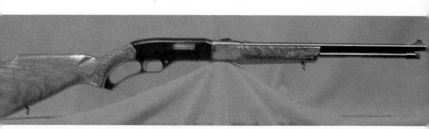

Winchester Model 250 De Luxe (above), Winchester Model 270 (below)

SMALL-BORE RIFLES

nence to lower-priced actions. Still fine models in this class are: Remington 572 (regular and light weights), Savage 29, Winchester 275 hammerless slide action (also in .22 WMR caliber and De Luxe model). Interest in Western Americana has encouraged the revival of several old lever-action designs, as well. Old favorite Marlin Model 39, long the only model in this field, is now rivaled by Marlin 56, Winchester 250 lever action, and Mossberg Palomino, each hammerless designs. Only the Marlin uses a clip-type magazine.

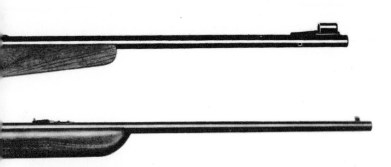

Marlin Model 56-Levermatic (top) is hammerless, has a clip magazine. Remington Model 510A Targetmaster can be used for small game, is best as a young shooter's target rifle

Winchester Model 250 (upper), a tubular-magazine rifle, handles all .22 cartridges. Remington Model 66 is fed through a tube in its nylon stock, holds 15 Long Rifle cartridges

No matter what action the shooter selects, the addition of sling swivels to support a sling can prove invaluable assets. These fit all models equally well, make carrying afield easier, and can be used advantageously by the shooter to steady his hold when firing. It is also important to remember always to fire against a solid background. This makes sense not only because it is easier to discern the target, but because the warning on the cartridge boxes reads, "Dangerous within a mile." It means exactly what it says.

35

With his Winchester 37 mounted, boy waits for instructor to throw bird

THE FIRST GUN

• Early training in shooting produces a skilled hunter in maturity. Young reflexes are fast and the youthful student has an open-minded approach to high-grade shooting techniques. If properly instructed, he will not acquire bad habits he must later unlearn. Training may begin whenever the child's co-ordination is up to it, always provided that adequate safety conditions exist and the instructor is qualified. Twelve years is a good average age at which to start. In any case, becoming a good shooter is a matter of experience and practice, whether with live ammunition on the target range or dry shooting in a basement or empty room.

The first arm should be a .22 rifle. The simpler it is, the better. The bolt-action, single-shot rifle is best. It

Raccoon looks curiously over shoulder. Below, Stevens Model 94Y

provides the new rifleman with the safest firearm he can own. Pump-actions are also good for the new shooter. If kept clean, they are most dependable. The .22 has the additional advantage of low report and recoil. There is no danger that the young shooter will develop a flinch, throwing his shots wide each time he fires. Later he can build up to more potent arms, gradually inuring himself to their strong kicks. Some manufacturers make a special short-stocked .22 single-shot rifle to encourage marksmanship at an early age. This is a vast improvement over the time when stocks had to be altered to accommodate young shooters. All of these new models are low in price (most of them under $35) and strong and accurate enough to permit the

THE FIRST GUN

learner to develop his marksmanship to a competent
degree. Some fine beginner's rifles in single-shot bolt-
action are: Marlin 101, Remington 510A, Marlin 15-Y,
Marlin 122 Junior Target, Harrington & Richardson
Pioneer 750 and Sahara 755 single-shot automatic,
which ejects and cocks, leaving action open for reloading. These models all weigh about 5½ pounds or
under. Beginner's models in single-shot, small-gauge
shotguns include the Winchester Model 37 in 20 gauge.
This is an excellent all-around small-game gun. Other
fine models are the Stevens 94Y in 20 or .410 gauge and
the Marlin-Glenfield Model 60-G in .410.

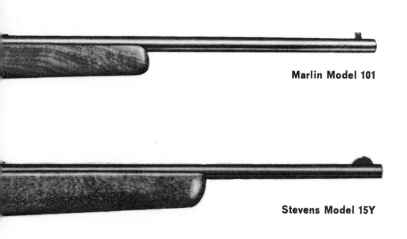

Marlin Model 101

Stevens Model 15Y

Savage Model 24DL shotgun

Harrington & Richardson Model 158 Topper

Marlin-Glenfield Model 60-G shotgun

WOODS RIFLES FOR DEER

• Few things prove more useful to the hunter than a knowledge of how to bag whitetail deer—by far the most numerous and widely distributed big game in America today. The elusive target it presents makes it choice for sport. The whitetail is seldom likely to expose himself in open areas to permit a clean shot, even at long range. Moving along runways, or feeding, he is constantly under cover.

The first rifle to snag the wary buck successfully and consistently was the old Kentucky. Light repeaters, such as the Winchester Model 1873, chambered for the .44-40 cartridge, soon followed, but these have long been obsolete. About fifty years ago, early models

Marlin Model 336-C (top) and Winchester Model 100

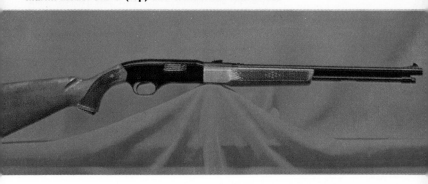

were supplanted by the Winchester .30-30, which is still effective for deer hunting, if bullets are well placed and the target is no more than 100 yards away. This model is sometimes good for beginners since it has a light recoil and allows him to shoot accurately without developing a "flinch." Modern rifles recoil sharply and it takes time for the new shooter to adjust himself to the jolt, so that he does not shoot wide of his mark each time he fires. However, as the modern rifle is more likely to provide a quick, humane killing punch, it is preferred to the old .30-30. As soon as possible, a shooter should spend several hours on a practice range, until he becomes reasonably efficient with the heavier arm. **41**

WOODS RIFLES FOR DEER

TARGET: Whitetail.

TERRAIN: Second-growth timber, heavy brush.

SHOOTING PROBLEMS: Hunter must take legal buck —although does may also be shot, depending on local conditions. As target will be moving, he must get off a quick, well-aimed first shot; he may not be permitted another chance. Ideally, the bullet should be placed within an eight-inch circle, directly behind the shoulder, well down into the chest, but several spots can be just as lethal. Deer approaching head-on should be hit at the neck-shoulder juncture or in mid-neck, just below the chin. When deer shows a side view, the hunter must aim just above the center of the neck, or just behind the elbow-point of the foreleg. A 100-grain bullet suits these purposes. Even when fairly well placed, the first hit often will not kill the animal, but merely fell or stun him, so a well-aimed follow-up shot is no less important and must be carried out quickly before the animal overcomes the shock of the first blow and escapes.

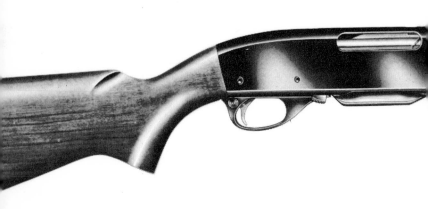

SHOOTING REQUIREMENTS: Super accuracy and great power are not required since 90 per cent of deer are shot at less than 100 yards, but a substantially heavy load with good brush-bucking power is needed for the thicketed terrain. A lightweight (not over 7½ pounds), short-barreled (no longer than 22 inches) rifle, equipped with a good sight that picks up in poor light, will permit the hunter to aim quickly and deliver a powerful, accurate blow. Yet it allows him to be ready for the follow-up if the first shot fails to down his deer. Several models fill the bill. Recommended are the Remington 760C carbine, with 18-inch barrel, the five-shot Winchester 100 autoloader, and the new five-shot Ruger carbine autoloader in .44 Magnum. Also good are: Winchester 88, Savage 99, and Marlin 336 (lever-models) and the Remington 742 autoloader. The best loads to consider for whitetail are: .308 Winchester, .358 Winchester, .270 Winchester, .35 Remington, .280 Remington, .300 Savage, all modern center-fire calibers.

Remington Model 760C Carbine—light, short barreled, high powered   **43**

LONG-RANGE SHOOTING

• Long-range shooting encompasses everything on open range from tramping after small game in farmlands to hunting big trophies in mountain areas. It includes three categories of shooting: big game, medium game, and varmints, in terrains where they can not be stalked closely, where, in some cases, an approach may take several days.

Ranges run from 200 yards up. A shooter who is on his mettle and well armed may even take a trophy at 1,000 yards. Strain is on both rifle and shooter to provide fine placement. Where prize trophies are involved, a guide is needed for advice and horses for packing the kill back to camp. Success—and enjoyment—largely depend on equipment: the proper arm, ammunition that performs well at high velocities and over long ranges, and powerful sights (at least a 4-power scope is needed, although the 6-power is a favorite among this class of hunter).

BIG GAME

The quest for prize trophies is a specialty of the advanced shooter. Conditions can be hazardous; a knowledge of the game is essential. The quarry is selected by its trophy value, although the meat from mountain sheep, moose, elk, caribou can be a savory by-product of the hunt. Once a prize is sighted, the hunter must be able to calculate the time for stalking, dispatching, retrieving, and dressing kill. A felled animal should not be left exposed overnight and retrieving may require scaling 1,000 yards of cliff.

.300 Weatherby Magnum De Luxe

Mountain goat is sure-footed but not especially
swift. Caribou (below, left) are fast movers. Right: Author
Koller with prize ram taken in Canadian Rockies

A potential prize trophy, bull elk roams through Montana timber

LONG-RANGE SHOOTING

TARGET: Rocky Mountain goat, mountain sheep, moose, elk, caribou.

TERRAIN: Craggy cliffs, mountains, and open plains.

SHOOTING PROBLEMS: Tough hides, heavy layers of fat, thick pelts complicate administering a fatal blow. Stalking may involve scaling and concealing oneself in dangerous rocky areas. Sheep have vision sharp enough to discern objects at one-half mile. Moose rely on hearing and scent for safety, to a lesser extent on sight. Elk and caribou depend on keen sense of smell. All can move rapidly. Goats are an exception; they are not so wary, concentrate on their immediate

Browning .375 Magnum Safari

surroundings, and never run fast, even when escaping hunter's fire. Usually, a hunter has ample time to judge range and wind drift and set himself for at least one shot with hold steady.

SHOOTING REQUIREMENTS: A rifle that takes a high-velocity cartridge and provides clean trigger-pull, a stock suited to shooting in prone or sitting positions, and full power at maximum range. Scopes aid in pinpoint placement. First choice of rifle—and cartridge—is the .300 Weatherby Magnum; second is the Winchester Model 70 Alaskan in .338 caliber. The .300 Holland & Holland Magnum cartridge offered in Winchester Model 70 and some Mauser types; Remington 700, Savage 110 and H. & R. bolt action, all in 7mm Magnum, are also fine. Winchester's new .264 Magnum cartridge in Model 70 can be used, but its 140-grain bullet lacks the punch needed and provided by the .30-caliber cartridge.

MEDIUM GAME

Antelope and mule-deer hunting is limited to the Far West—extensive, open country where distances covered in tracking are great. Many chase the herds by Jeep, but a true sportsman leaves transportation nearby to stalk his prey on foot.

TARGET: Antelope, mule deer.

TERRAIN: Usually open plains, though mule deer is at home in sparsely timbered foothills, mountains.

SHOOTING PROBLEMS: Both animals are alert. Antelope can move at 60 miles per hour when pressed. **47**

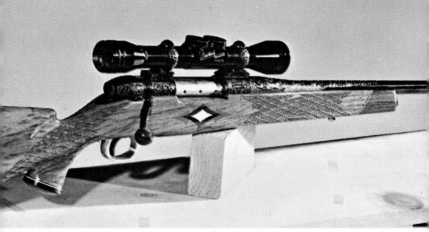
Customized Weatherby Magnum with scope, inlaid stock

LONG-RANGE SHOOTING

Hunter must approach prey cautiously, hugging ground, taking advantage of any cover. He will probably be prone or sitting when he sights and shoots. His first shot must be accurate. He seldom gets a second, and he must calculate for a long-range shot and probably for a moving target.

SHOOTING REQUIREMENTS: With no foliage interference, small calibers with lightweight bullets buck wind and hold killing punch over long ranges. Their high muzzle velocity provides an almost flat trajectory, minimizing errors in range judgment. Best are: .257, 7-mm, .270 Weatherby Magnums. Also effective are: .280 Remington; .300 Holland & Holland; .270, .243, .308 Winchester; .264 Winchester Magnum, and the .30-06 with 150-grain bullet. Speed is unimportant, so bolt-actions with added weight of full stocks and long barrels aid shooting. Choose Weatherby rifles, Savage Premier 110, Winchester 70, Remington 700, or Mauser types.

48

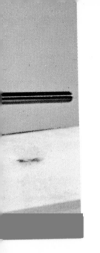

Pronghorn antelope (also below, left)

Small herd of elk

Remington Model 700 De Luxe

Remington Model 760ADL

Remington Model 742ADL

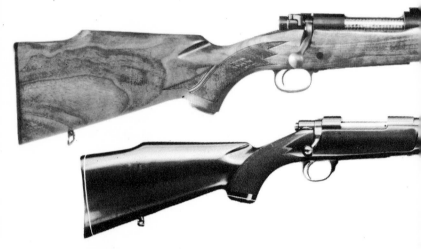

LONG-RANGE SHOOTING

VARMINTS

Varmint hunting keeps eye and reflexes in trim and provides year-around practice in long-range shooting with a light gun and fitted scope. Seldom restricted by game laws, it reduces the pest population of animals and birds that have little or no value as food or fur, but prey upon animals and crops that do.

TARGET: Gopher, prairie dog, chuck, coyote, bobcat, mountain lion, crow, hawk, great horned owl. (Predatory birds may be protected; check local game laws.)

TERRAIN: Open farm country or prairies.

SHOOTING PROBLEMS: Target is small, wary, and clever with acute hearing and excellent vision. Hunter should approach carefully, using any available cover. Birds must be bagged when perched. Once in flight, they are almost impossible to hit with a rifle.

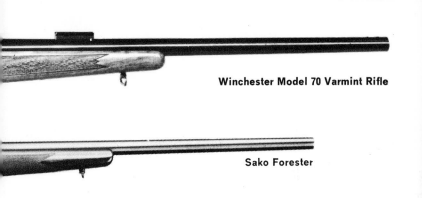

Winchester Model 70 Varmint Rifle

Sako Forester

Proud youngster displays chuck bagged with Winchester 67

Wolverine (top) and grey fox are cunning marauders

Watchful, predatory bobcat

Woodchuck: menace to agriculture

Savage/Anschutz Model 153

SHOOTING REQUIREMENTS: Precision of big-game rifle without its potency and a bullet that can sustain killing power and expand rapidly on impact. Top load is regular .222 Remington, firing a 50-grain bullet. For targets within 100 yards, the .22 Winchester Magnum rim-fire, firing 40-grain, hollow-point load is fine. Rifles: Mossberg Model 640-K, bolt action; Marlin Model 57-M, lever action; Winchester Model 275, slide action; single-shot Colteer—all chambered for .22 WMR—and Remington Model 600, Savage 340, Sako, BSA—bolt actions chambered for .222 Remington. For unusually long ranges use: .225 or .243 Winchester Varmint or regular Model 70, Savage Model 110, Browning Safari, Remington Model 700 (all three in .22-250 caliber), or one of the Mauser bolt actions.

53

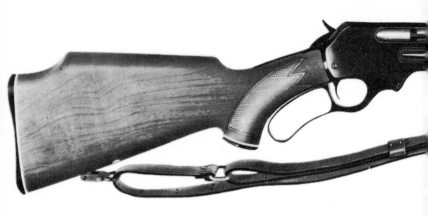

BIG GAME IN TIMBER

• Many of the same animals pursued by the long-range shooter may also be found in timber country, but the shooting requirements and equipment must be suitable to the different conditions. Ranges are variable, but generally shorter than those encountered in open country. They go up to 300 yards, but a moving animal may have to be taken at under 50, so super-accuracy is not so important as speed. A trip to the Rockies or the Far North where such game may be found demands much pre-planning, equipping properly for the hunt, and reserving camp and horses in advance.

TARGET: Moose, elk, caribou, bison (buffalo), black and grizzly bear, Alaskan brown bear and giant moose.

TERRAIN: Remote areas of West, Northwest; high mountain country; heavy, wild brush and timber; Alaskan coastal regions for bear.

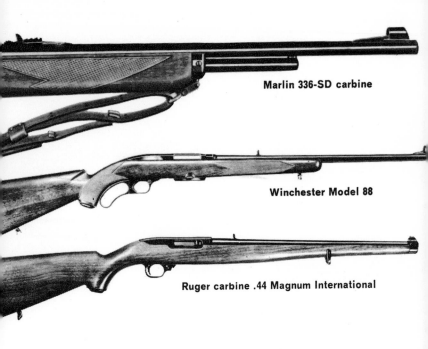

Marlin 336-SD carbine

Winchester Model 88

Ruger carbine .44 Magnum International

SHOOTING PROBLEMS: Wary animals with keen sense of smell, good hearing and vision. They must be stalked skillfully, ideally upwind. Some knowledge of the target's habits is essential. Bear are scarce, usually travel alone, and move swiftly (sometimes 20 miles per day). They should be hunted in fall near feeding areas or in spring as hibernation ends. Aroused bear, especially grizzly, is dangerous and swift. The first shot should be sure, striking brain, smashing spine, or smashing shoulder and striking heart. A miss can be fatal; the wise hunter has the next cartridge in the chamber. Elk, caribou, and moose are more difficult to spot in timber regions than in open country. Their brownish-grey pelts hide them in shadows of tree trunks, leaf patterns, and autumn grasses. They move soundlessly and are highly sensitive to intruders. **55**

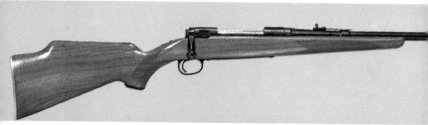

Savage 110-MC (above) and Savage 99 De Luxe

For grizzly bear (below) .308-caliber cartridge is minimum load

Coloring protects elk (below). Moose relies on ears, nose

BIG GAME IN TIMBER

American bison are protected by game laws in most areas except Montana, Wyoming, and Alberta. Texas permits shooting males over 10 years and steers. Arizona holds an annual hunt open to 50 sportsmen.

SHOOTING REQUIREMENTS: The hunter should use the most powerful arm he can handle quickly and shoot accurately under stress of a charge. A powerful rifle, delivering a heavy, controlled-expansion bullet, is necessary to cut tough hide, pelt, and bone. Topping the list of fast-firing, quick-handling timber rifles is Remington Model 760 slide-action in .30-06 Springfield, .280 Remington, .270 Winchester. In the same calibers, Remington's 742 autoloader (slightly heavier than the 760) is a fine arm. Both are available in .308 cartridge which is one of the best current timber loads. Also good are three lever actions: The Marlin 336-SD, Winchester Model 88, and Savage 99-EG, which latter is available both in .308 and the heavy .358 calibers. Many bolt actions take the necessary big-game loads: Remington 600 carbine in .308 and 600 Magnum carbine in .350 Remington Magnum, Winchester 70, Remington 700, Savage 110 (right- and left-hand), and a few Mausers. Fastest of all is the new Winchester Model 100 autoloader, firing .308 cartridges.

Marlin 336 Magnum in .444 Marlin

Remington Model 600 Magnum carbine

Alaskan brown bear eating salmon at creek edge

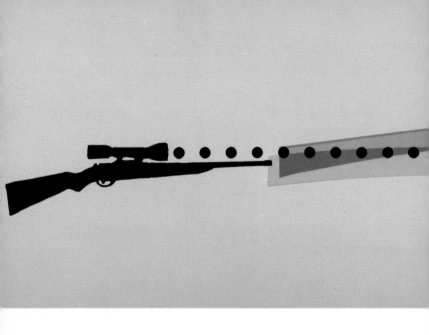

SIGHTING THE RIFLE

• It is an axiom among riflemen that "no rifle is better than its sights," but sights are helpful only if properly aligned. Seldom does a rifle come from the factory or shop sighted-in and ready for use, and too few shooters are able to recognize or correct the defect.

The principles of sighting are simple: the line of sight must be parallel to the line of bore, and sight elevation should take bullet trajectory into account. The first adjustment is for windage. The sight is moved to right or left in the direction the bullet must go to eliminate any discrepancy between the actual striking point and the desired striking point. For example, if a group of five shots, fired from a rifle steadied in position and aimed at target center, hits six inches left of center, the rear sight must be moved to the right to

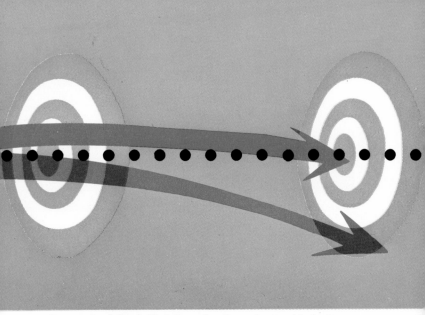

A properly sighted rifle takes advantage of natural trajectory

correct the error. On micrometer, or scope, sights, this is done in graduated ½-minute (sometimes ¼-minute, sometimes minute) clicks, each click producing a ¼-inch movement at 50 yards, ½-inch movement at 100 yards, one-inch movement at 200 yards. (A ¼-minute click produces a ¼-inch movement at 100 yards; a one-minute click a one-inch movement at 100 yards.)

Adjusting open iron sights in dovetail barrel slots (usually provided by the manufacturer) is more difficult and necessarily a matter of trial and error. Before making any adjustment, it is wise to draw a line of reference from the front edge of the sight base to the rifle barrel. A flat brass punch and hammer may be used to tap the sight in the correcting direction. To check the adjusted alignment, a second group must **61**

Mykrom Scope Mount

Williams matted front-ramp sight cuts glare

SIGHTING THE RIFLE

be fired. If the amount of movement has not been sufficient, the reference line should again be consulted and the sight tapped until the difference is eliminated.

Errors in elevation are corrected in a similar manner. In a rifle that shoots low, the rear sight must be raised; if it shoots high, the rear sight must be lowered. In micrometer and scope sights, there is a second dial by which adjustments can be made in ¼-minute, ½-minute, or minute clicks on the same basis as corrections are made for windage. Open iron sights are adjusted by tapping. There is one exception to this relatively simple pattern. Occasionally a rifle will shoot high when the rear sight is set as low as it will go and cannot be lowered. In such cases, a higher front sight must be installed which, in effect, lowers the muzzle.

The most difficult problem a shooter encounters in sighting a rifle is discovering its point-blank range.

Unusual for shotguns is Williams ramp sight
(above, left) which raises sighting level, improves accuracy.
Scale on Williams 5D receiver, or peep, sight (right)
simplifies adjustments for wind, elevation

That is, the range at which no calculation for trajectory is necessary when taking aim: a bullet directed at target center, hits target center. Point-blank range differs with cartridges and with variations in bullet weights and shapes in the same cartridge. To determine it properly, experimentation on the target range and a study of ballistic charts is necessary. Knowledge of a rifle's point-blank range is important for it relieves the shooter of complex calculations. A bullet as it is discharged rises slightly, then follows a gently sloping trajectory. If a high-velocity long-range rifle, such as the Winchester Westerner, is sighted in at 100 yards, the bullet path shows an exaggerated drop at longer ranges (eight inches below aim at 250 yards). Yet the same rifle sighted-in at 250 yards shows only a slight rise in bullet flight between 50 and 250 yards, shooting about 2.5 inches above point of aim at 100 yards, two

63

Lyman Targetspot scope on custom Sako rifle aids benchrest shooter

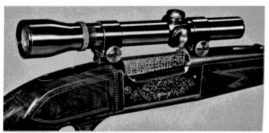

K-3 Weaver scope on Savage Model 99

SIGHTING THE RIFLE

inches at 200 yards, and hitting on target at 250 yards.
• Three types of sights are available. The shooter's
choice depends on price, what feels comfortable to
him, and the type of shooting he expects to do.

SCOPE: By far the best sighting device available,
although it is fairly expensive, adds bulk and weight to
the rifle, and is almost useless in rain, fog, or snow.
At dusk, dawn, or on hazy days, when it would be difficult to fix iron sights on target, the scope's light-gathering qualities permit greater accuracy. Its aiming

K-1 Weaver scope on Remington Model 11-48 shotgun

J-25 Weaver scope on Remington Model 572

devices—dot, cross hair, post—and magnification simplify the shooter's problems and present a clear image.

Deciding how much power to use is often a problem when choosing a scope, but usually this is determined by game and terrain. In timber regions, where game is moving and at moderate ranges, low-power scopes (3X or less) which provide wider fields of vision are best. In open country, where game generally is not moving and ranges are long, high-power scopes (6X or 8X) with greater magnification are more suitable.

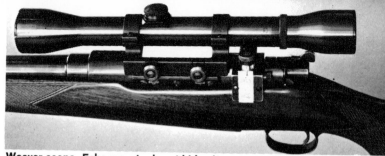
Weaver scope, Echo mount, almost hide alternate receiver sight

SIGHTING THE RIFLE

PEEP SIGHT: Less expensive than scopes and far more durable, the peep rates second among sights. The proximity of eye to sight permits an unusually wide field of vision, and the eye's instinctive ability to peer through the small aperture, automatically centering the front sight, increases the chances of accuracy. Since the hunter needs only to align the front sight with the game, the peep is far faster to use than open-rear sights which have three points of reference: rear sight, front sight, and game.

OPEN REAR SIGHT: Ranking third in performance, but by far the least expensive, are open iron sights. They are rugged, easy travelers, and on bright days give an unobstructed view of the target, permitting the hunter to shoot tight (to keep his shot-groups within a small circular area). With no light-gathering properties, they are almost useless when light is bad, and focusing with them is extremely slow. The shooter's eye must center the front sight in the rear sight, then align the front sight with the game. The difficulty of the process is often increased because light striking the front sight tends to produce a halo on one or the other side of it. As the eye attempts to center the sight, it is likely to misjudge what is actual and what is illusory. This can sometimes be eliminated by placing a hood over the front sight to standardize the light.

BALLISTICS CHART

FOR PRINCIPAL CENTER-FIRE CARTRIDGES

MUZZLE VELOCITY is a measure in feet per second of the time required for a bullet to travel from muzzle to a point 75 feet away.
MUZZLE ENERGY is a calculation in foot pounds of the force exerted by a bullet as it leaves the muzzle. It is a rough measurement of the comparative killing power of cartridges.
MID-RANGE TRAJECTORY is the number of inches a bullet rises above the line of bore, at the range specified.

CARTRIDGE	BULLET Wt. Grs.	VELOCITY Muzzle	ENERGY Muzzle	MID-RANGE TRAJECTORY 100 yds.	200 yds.
.219 ZIPPER	56	3110	1200	0.6	2.9
.22 HORNET	45	2690	720	0.8	4.3
.222 REMINGTON	50	3200	1140	0.5	2.5
.220 SWIFT	48	4110	1800	0.3	1.4
.243 WINCHESTER	100	3070	2090	0.5	2.2
.250 SAVAGE	100	2820	1760	0.6	2.9
.257 ROBERTS	100	2900	1870	0.6	2.7
.257 ROBERTS	117	2650	1820	0.7	3.4
.270 WINCHESTER	100	3580	2840	0.4	1.7
.270 WINCHESTER	130	3140	2840	0.5	2.1
.280 REMINGTON	150	2810	2630	0.6	2.6
.30-30 WINCHESTER	150	2410	1930	0.9	4.2
.30-30 WINCHESTER	170	2220	1860	1.2	4.6
.30 REMINGTON	170	2220	1860	1.2	4.6
.30-06 SPRINGFIELD	110	3420	2850	0.4	2.1
.30-06 SPRINGFIELD	180	2700	2910	0.7	2.9
.30-06 SPRINGFIELD	220	2410	2830	0.8	3.9
.300 SAVAGE	150	2670	2370	0.7	3.2
.300 SAVAGE	180	2370	2240	0.9	3.7
.300 H.& H. MAGNUM	180	2920	3400	0.6	2.4
.300 H.& H. MAGNUM	220	2620	3350	0.7	3.1
.32 WINCHESTER SPECIAL	170	2280	1960	1.0	4.8
.32 REMINGTON	170	2220	1860	1.0	4.9
.348 WINCHESTER	200	2530	2840	0.8	3.8
.348 WINCHESTER	250	2350	3060	0.9	4.4
.358 WINCHESTER	200	2530	2840	0.8	3.6
.358 WINCHESTER	250	2250	2810	1.0	4.4
.35 REMINGTON	200	2210	2170	1.1	5.2
.375 H.& H. MAGNUM	270	2740	4500	0.7	2.9
.375 H.& H. MAGNUM	300	2550	4330	0.7	3.3

THE SHOTGUN

PART 3

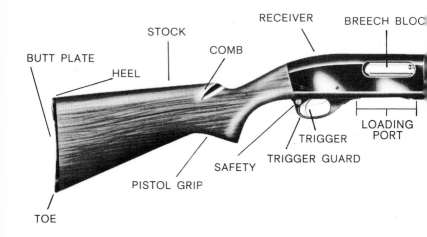

RECEIVER   BREECH BLOC[K]

STOCK

BUTT PLATE   COMB

HEEL

LOADING PORT

TRIGGER

TRIGGER GUARD

SAFETY

PISTOL GRIP

TOE

WHAT MAKES A SHOTGUN

• The versatility of the shotgun makes it the most widely used hunter's arm in America. Loaded with the finest size of shot, it kills quail, woodcock, doves, and snipe. Increase the shot size and it is ready for duck, grouse, pheasant, and rabbit. With the heaviest birdshot, it takes geese, foxes, turkeys, bobcats, and other large varmints. Loaded with a rifled slug, it takes deer almost as well as the rifle. Its major limitation is a relatively short maximum effective range of about 75 yards.

The design of the shotgun is simple. The barrel is made of soft steel, thin walled and smoothbored. An enlargement at the breech end of the bore—the chamber—contains the shell. When the trigger is pulled, it releases the firing pin which moves sharply forward and strikes the rear end of the shell, detonating the primer and thus firing the charge. The break-open single-shot is the simplest model. The breech is hinged

70

Preceding pages: Winchester Model 59

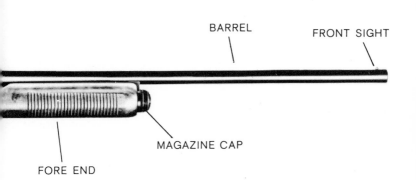

BARREL

FRONT SIGHT

MAGAZINE CAP

FORE END

to permit efficient loading and extraction of the shell.

A shotgun must throw a load of shot in an evenly spread pattern at fairly short range. It is pointed, not aimed, and speed and easy handling are essential. This gun has no rear sight, so the eye of the shooter must take its place. The stock is designed to give full support to the cheek, putting the shooter's eye in the same relationship to the breech from shot to shot.

The killing range of the shotgun is limited to the distance at which the target cannot escape through the pattern without sustaining hits from enough pellets to kill quickly. The difference in this "killing pattern" spread is roughly five yards between gauges when they are firing loads of comparable value. What the 12 does at 60 yards, the 16 does at 55, the 20 at 50. The smaller 28 and .410 gauges fall below this average. Their maximum effective range is 35 yards.

Pump action, showing the pump
(lower right) pulled back. The carrier is
picking up shell from the magazine

ACTIONS AND HOW THEY WORK

• Shotguns are made in five action types: single shot, double barrel, pump, autoloader, and bolt action. They were once made in lever action, but these have been discontinued. The single-shot, single-barreled shotgun is the simplest and least expensive type.

DOUBLES: The first multiple-shot gun was a twin-tubed model capable of firing two shots. The modern double gun has been refined and improved, but the classic design remains. It is really two guns, side by side, with one stock. In addition to dual barrels, it has twin lock systems (actions) and usually two triggers.

OVER/UNDER DOUBLES: This is a more modern version of the side-by-side double barrel. It has the added advantage of a single sighting-plane. Many shooters find it difficult to sight over the twin barrels of a regular double gun. They tend to "cross-fire" over the barrels rather than sight properly down the center rib. With an over/under, the gunner sights along the top barrel. Some shooters feel the vertical arrangement of the barrels prevents tipping or canting to one side which frequently causes a miss.

PUMP OR SLIDE-ACTION GUNS: The pump was the first repeating shotgun developed in this country that is still produced today. The shells—a maximum of six—are contained in a tubular magazine below the single barrel. After firing, the slide handle is jerked backward to eject the empty shell case and recock the hammer. As the slide handle is pushed forward a fresh shell is lifted from the magazine and carried into the chamber. The final forward movement of the slide handle locks the breech block and the gun is ready to fire again.

AUTO- OR SELF-LOADERS: As the term implies, the self-loader loads itself after each shot and the shooter has only to pull the trigger to fire the gun each time. The magazine is tubular, as in the slide-action gun. Two autoloader systems are currently used: the recoil system, which utilizes the energy imparted by the backward pressure of the fired shell, and the gas system, which takes a part of the expanding powder gases through a small vent in the bore. The gas operates a piston which, in turn, opens the breech, thus ejecting the empty case, recocking the hammer, and feeding a fresh load into the chamber.

BOLT ACTIONS: Simple and inexpensive, the bolt action is also the slowest repeating shotgun to operate. Shells are carried either in a tubular magazine or in a box magazine, usually detachable, directly forward of the trigger guard. To eject a fired case or prepare the gun for loading, the bolt handle is lifted and pulled back to the rear of the receiver. Pushing the handle forward picks up a fresh shell. Turning the bolt into the locked position cocks the action and closes it.

Cutaway of buckshot load

.410 bore— .410″

28 gauge— .550″

20 gauge— .615″

16 gauge—.670″

12 gauge—.73

SHOTGUN GAUGES AND SHELLS

• A shotgun's gauge—like a rifle's caliber—is a measure of its bore diameter. The standard of measurement, however, is an odd one. It is the number of balls, each fitting the bore exactly, that can be produced from one pound of lead. The number of balls weighing one pound that fit the bore of a 12-gauge gun will, then, total twelve. The only exception to this is the little .410, which is measured in thousandths of an inch. Shotshells are made up of powder, shot, and primer. When the gun is fired, the primer ignites, firing the powder, which propels the shot. The case is usually made of paper with a brass head. Remington, however, has recently produced a new case made of polyethylene plastic, with a steel head coated with copper and brass. This SP Premier Grade shell (12 gauge only) seems the most durable, waterproof shell yet made.

74

Cutaway of rifled-slug shell

10 gauge—.775"

Cutaway of standard load

The longer the shell, the more shot pellets it can contain; the higher the shot-size number, the smaller the pellets. A rifled-slug shell would compare in size to a .70-caliber bullet and is used only for big game.

Range and the size of the target are the factors that fix the shot load used. For small game birds, such as quail or woodcock, at fairly short range, the 12-gauge gun can be effectively loaded with a shell carrying three drams of powder (equivalent) [shell manufacturers do not reveal the actual measure they use] and 1⅛ ounces of #9 shot. For larger birds, the 12's load can be increased to 3¾ drams (equivalent) of powder and 1¼ ounces of #6 shot. The 12 gauge will also take Magnum shells for ducks at long range, and buckshot or a one-ounce rifled slug for big game. Smaller gauges carry proportionately smaller loads.

75

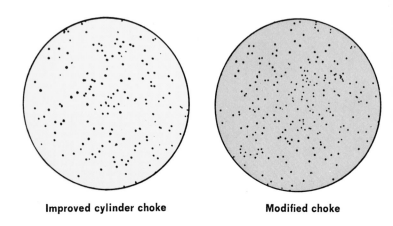

Improved cylinder choke   Modified choke

CHOKES AND PATTERNS

• The choke of a shotgun barrel works in much the same way as the nozzle of a hose. When the nozzle is tightened, a fine stream of water is projected far out. As the nozzle is opened, the spray pattern becomes wider and travels a shorter distance. The amount of water coming through the hose does not change; only the width of the opening it goes through. In the same way, a shot pattern is changed by narrowing the size of the bore near the muzzle.

All shotguns are made with one choke boring or another. These range from the standard three—full, modified, and improved cylinder—to the adjustable choke which can be attached to the barrel and permits the shooter to change choke in the field. The effective shooting range in a choke boring is determined by the distance at which at least 60 per cent of the shot

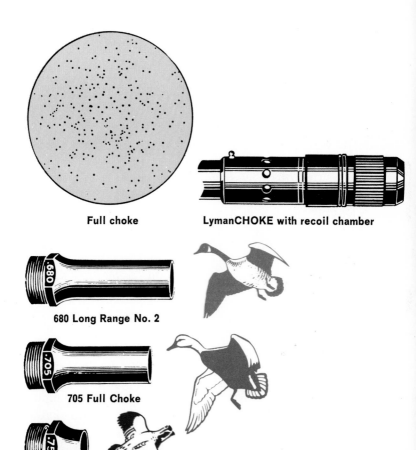

Full choke

LymanCHOKE with recoil chamber

680 Long Range No. 2

705 Full Choke

755 Tube

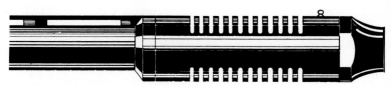

Cutts Compensator

pellets will fall within a 30-inch circle. This is about 25 yards for improved cylinder, 35 yards for modified, and 40 yards for full choke. For normally predictable ranges the following chokes are recommended:

IMPROVED CYLINDER: Rabbit, quail, woodcock, grouse, skeet shooting.

MODIFIED: Ruffed grouse, pheasant, doves, ducks over decoys.

FULL CHOKE: Waterfowl pass shooting, turkey, geese, foxes, trapshooting.

Double guns offer the advantage of two chokes, one for the first shot at close range, the second ready for a follow-up if the first is missed. The usual combinations are: right barrel modified, left barrel full; or right barrel improved cylinder, left modified. Skeet guns are also made with less choke in the right barrel. Trap guns and doubles used for longer ranges have both barrels bored full choke.

It is not necessary to have a multitude of guns to hunt different kinds of game. The shooter can decide what choke he will need most and get a gun that can be fitted with interchangeable barrels. Many manufacturers provide these at fairly low cost. The disadvantage here is that changing over from one set of choked barrels to another cannot be done on the spur of the moment. A more convenient answer is an adjustable choke on a single-barreled gun. With this device the shooter can obtain any degree of choke. Because of its raised surface, some shooters also use the adjustable choke as a front sighting aid. Recoil-reducers are incorporated in certain models; others, like the Cutts Compensator, are basically recoil-reducers combined with interchangeable choke tubes.

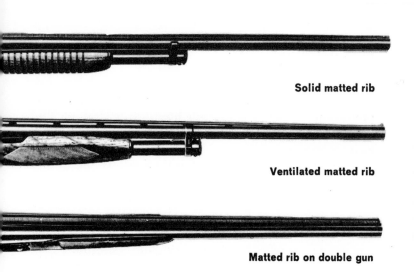

Solid matted rib

Ventilated matted rib

Matted rib on double gun

BARRELS AND RIBS

• The standard barrel lengths are 26, 28, 30, and 32 inches. Generally speaking, the longer barrels are used in wildfowl shooting. Shorter barrels usually are used in heavy brush country for convenience in handling.

A rib is frequently attached to the barrel of a shotgun. These are either solid or ventilated, with a matted surface for easy sighting. Matting prevents reflection and glare, and the raised surface of the rib acts as a better sighting plane than the barrel itself. The ventilated rib is particularly useful for repeated firing over an extended period, as in trapshooting. Heat waves rising from the barrel will cause a mirage leading to inaccurate shooting. The ventilated rib permits some of this heat to come out of slots in the surface of the barrel, and channels it out to the sides.

UPLAND GUNS

• Upland game birds can rise from dense cover at speeds of 30 to 50 miles per hour, so a shotgun that handles quickly and easily is the first requirement for upland hunting. The shot must be made during the brief, flashing glances the hunter gets of his quarry before it soars or runs out of sight and range.

Several factors determine the choice of gauge used: size and speed of target, the terrain, and whether or not the shooter works with a dog. Most upland game can be taken with a 20- or a 16-gauge shotgun; a 12 gauge may blow a small bird to bits. The 12-gauge proves most valuable when hunting larger birds, such as the wild turkey. For grouse and woodcock in densely thicketed New England, the open-choked 20 gauge is deadly, while in the more open country of the South and West, the hunter chooses a 16 or 12 gauge for longer shots at quail, partridge, and pheasant. If the hunter uses a dog, the range can be fairly accurately determined in advance, depending on the breed and ability of the dog. A good bird dog usually holds the

**Winchester Model 21 custom
(and expensive) double gun**

Ruffed grouse

bird at point at a known, reasonably close distance each time. Thus, the hunter has only to add this fairly constant factor to his own distance from the dog to get a good estimate of the shooting range.

If the shooter is working alone, the bird may flush underfoot, or run 30 or 40 yards before taking flight. In this case, the long range of a 12 gauge makes it the preferred gun. It also offers a better opportunity to make a clean kill, thus lessening the chance of crippling birds and losing them in the underbrush, where they are difficult to recover without a dog.

Upland guns weigh from 5¾ to 7½ pounds and a pound one way or the other may mean an important loss or gain of time for the hunter to get on target.

TARGET: Grouse, pheasant, partridge, woodcock, quail, wild turkey.

TERRAIN: Grouse: rolling timberland and low valley cover. Pheasant: farmland for feed, low growth or swampland for cover. Partridge: stubble fields, open prairie, occasionally desert. Woodcock: low, moist ground, heavy cover. Quail: dry ground vegetation, usually low. Wild turkey: deep woods, morasses, swampland, and thicketed mountain country.

SHOOTING PROBLEMS: Fast-moving, extremely wary quarry in close cover, with ranges of 20 to 50 yards. Fast action is needed to hit target before it disappears.

Possible mutilation of game from a too-heavy load must be avoided. (Wild turkey is the exception; being large and heavy, it requires a heavier charge of powder and shot.) Maximum patience and endurance is exacted from the hunter.

SHOOTING REQUIREMENTS: Lightest, shortest gun that carries a suitable shot load. Fast action is a must. The choice of pump or autoloader in a repeater is individual, but double guns, although limited to two shots without reloading, are slightly faster and better balanced. Their two-choke option also permits a follow-up shot at longer range and their shorter over-all length is an asset. In repeaters, the additional length of the receiver that houses the firing mechanism must be included in over-all measurements, making a repeater several inches longer than a double of the same barrel length. Twenty-six inches is the suggested maximum barrel length for upland gunning.

RECOMMENDED GUNS: A light 20-gauge shotgun is recommended as closest to an ideal upland bird gun, but it requires a high degree of speed from the hunter. The 20 and 16 gauges chambered for Express and Magnum loads have challenged the first-place position held by heavier gauges. A 20 kills neatly up to 50 yards without mutilating the game, handles easily and quickly in close cover. Choice upland guns in-

Browning Superposed Grade V

Fox Model B-ST

Ringneck pheasant

In the field.   Woodcock (below)

Grouse (above)

Bobwhite quail (below)

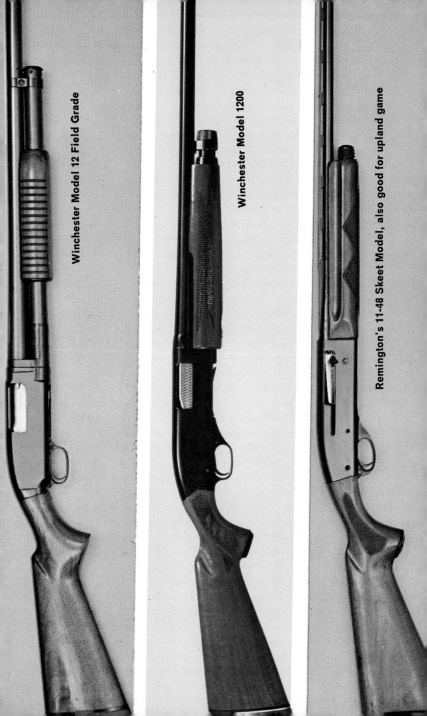

Winchester Model 12 Field Grade

Winchester Model 1200

Remington's 11-48 Skeet Model, also good for upland game

Charles Daly Model 500

clude: **Doubles**—Winchester Model 21, custom-made only, priced from $1,200 up. Fox Model B, somewhat on the heavy side, but modestly priced and reliable. Browning Superposed over/under is a top-grade Belgian gun assembled here. Dakin over/under 20-gauge Model 147 Magnum can drop birds at 50 yards. **Pump Guns**—Winchester Model 1200 in either 12 or 20 gauge, High Standard Flite-King Field in 12, 20 or .410 gauge, also the Mossberg Model 500 furnished in 12, 16 or 20 gauge. Featherweight Ithaca Model 37 is 5¾ pounds in 20 gauge. Savage Model 30 weighs six pounds in 20 gauge, seven in 12 gauge. Stevens Model 77 is virtually the same as the Model 30. Remington Model 870 weighs about 6½ pounds in 20 gauge. **Autoloaders**—Winchester Model 59 has Win-Lite fiberglass barrel, comes in 12 gauge only, weighs 6½ pounds. Winchester 1400 in 12 or 20 gauge weighs seven pounds. Regular Remington Model 11-48 weighs 6½ pounds in 20 gauge. Most shotguns come in three or four gauges, many are chambered for Express and Magnum loads. **Extras**—A matted rib helps eliminate glare and gives flat-plane sighting. However, it adds a quarter of a pound to the average pump and auto-

Ithaca 37R De Luxe repeater

Wild turkey in protective foliage

UPLAND GUNS

loader. An adjustable choke enables the gunner to change the shot pattern, yet adds no extra weight, as a section of the barrel is removed to allow for the choke attachment.

Relatively few shotgunners today are one-gun hunters. Many have a bird gun and a duck gun, which most often means a 20 gauge and a 12 gauge. Actually, the 20 gauge comes closer, in the Magnum chamberings, to filling the needs of the upland gunner than the average 12 gauge. A light 20 makes an ideal upland bird gun for hunting in close cover. The lightest gun that holds the necessary shot load is always the preferable choice.

WILDFOWL GUNS

• Wild ducks and geese, with their heavy feather covering, are tough birds to kill. A wildfowl gunner must shoot a tight pattern and place a minimum of five or six shot into the bird to kill it in the air. In decoy shooting, where the bird flies in over the decoys near the shooter's blind, ranges are likely to be 40 yards or less. The more difficult pass shooting, attempted as the target flies high overhead, offers the longest-range shooting of any shotgun sport.

Wildfowl gunning demands more precision in pointing than upland shooting. The longer range makes the target seem smaller. Skill is needed to determine the proper lead—the distance the gunner must point ahead of the target to allow for the bird's movement and the speed of the shot. Because of the heavy shot requirements, any gun lighter than a 12 gauge is a handicap to the gunner and frequently results in crippled birds. Since easy handling and the necessary power can be built into pumps and autoloaders, these have been the first choice of wildfowlers for over fifty years. Very few doubles are produced in this country. There are,

Savage Model 775

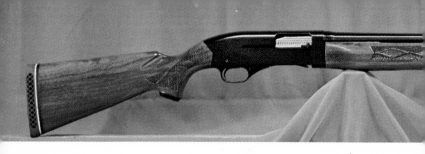

WILDFOWL GUNS

however, many fine imported doubles available.
TARGET: Wild ducks, geese.
TERRAIN: Marshland.
SHOOTING PROBLEMS: Pass shooting—No shotgun is too big for pass shooting. The target is moving at high speed—60 or 70 miles per hour—and can come from any direction. The shotgunner must know the correct lead for every range up to the limit of his gun's reach. He must be able to judge the angle and speed of the target and allow for any variations that wind might cause. **Decoy shooting**—Correct type, number, and placement of decoys for the various species of ducks, and how to use a duck call effectively are important techniques to be learned. Proper concealment

92

Winchester Model 1400

**Remington Model 870
with ventilated rib**

Browning Double Automatic Standard

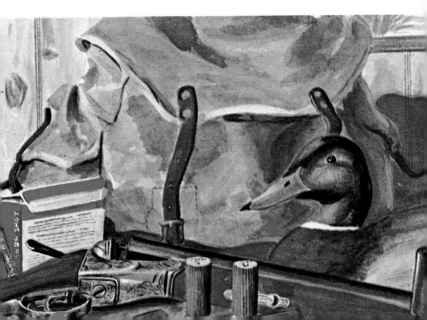

Decoy shooting from natural blind

WILDFOWL GUNS

in a blind, the maneuverability of the gun, and the size of the charge are the other major considerations.

Blinds may be made in many ways and of many different types of material. The natural ones, made of grasses and reeds found on the spot, are best, but difficult to assemble permanently. No matter what the blind, the most important thing for the hunter to remember is to keep his head down and remain absolutely motionless.

SHOOTING REQUIREMENTS: A fairly heavy—about 7½ pounds—single-tube repeating gun with a minimum barrel length of 28 inches is appropriate. Both of these factors aid accuracy in swinging and pointing. Also helpful is a matted rib. The elevated, non-glaring flat

Winchester Model 1200 Magnum Duck Gun

Remington Model 870 Magnum AP

Savage Model 30-ACL left-hand pump

surface gives better control in sighting. The adjustable choke—optional on many current pump and autoloading guns—is useful. This sets the bore for close-range shots (up to 40 yards) when birds charge in at decoys, or for full choke to give tighter patterns necessary for pass shooting.

RECOMMENDED GUNS: Pass shooting—A 12-gauge Magnum, firing a load of 1⅞ ounces, will give dependable kills on ducks at 70 yards, geese at 60 yards. These are heavy guns—well over eight pounds—made in the following models: Remington 1100 Magnum, Winchester 1200 12-gauge Magnum Duck Gun, Stevens 77-M, Savage Model 775, and Browning Superposed Magnum over/under. All should be purchased with full-

95

choke barrels. **Decoy shooting**—Winchester Model 1200 pump, Winchester Model 1400 autoloader, Remington 11-48 auto, Remington 870 pump, High Standard Supermatic, Savage Model 30 pump (also made in left-handed action), Stevens Model 77, Browning Automatic 5, and Browning Double Automatic (two-shot) are all good choices in 12 gauge. Loaded with the 2³/₄-inch Magnum shell, they are fast enough to handle well over decoying ducks and have enough range for some conservative pass shooting—up to 60 yards.

Hutchins' goose breeds in Arctic, migrates through Midwest

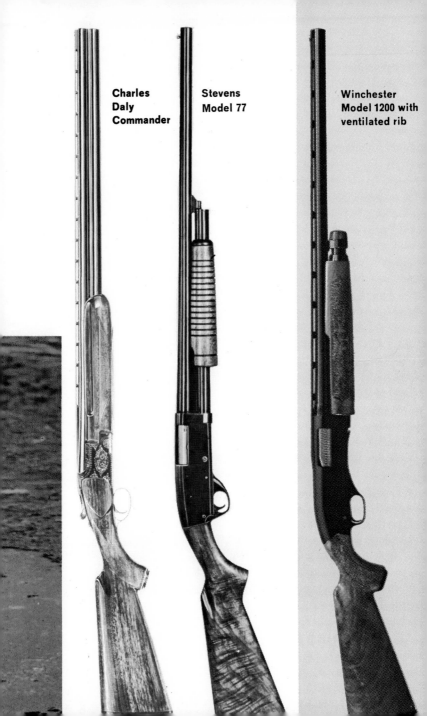

Charles
Daly
Commander

Stevens
Model 77

Winchester
Model 1200 with
ventilated rib

Fiberglass being processed at Winchester

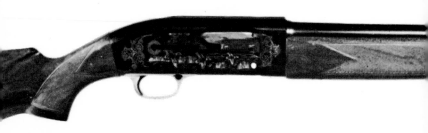

Five hundred miles of glass filament are used in the Win-Lite barrel

FIBERGLASS BARRELS

• Increasing the strength of the shotgun barrel without adding to the weight has always plagued the gun designer. Winchester's Model 59 autoloader has been made with a revolutionary new barrel called the "Win-Lite," which is made of fiberglass. Several layers of fiberglass cloth are wrapped over a very thin-walled steel tube that has been pre-wound with miles of fiberglass filaments. It is then heat cured, ground to size, and finished. The result is a barrel twice as strong as a comparable one in steel, yet only half as heavy. It won't heat up and is not affected by exposure to weather. And if, under extraordinary conditions, the barrel should blow up, there is no fragmentation as occasionally happens with steel.

Winchester Model 59 automatic with Win-Lite barrel

THE HANDGUN

PART 4

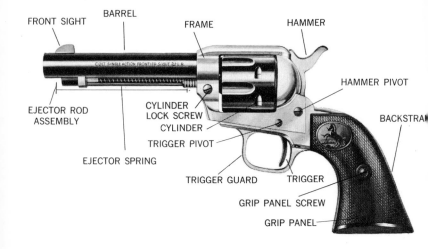

FRONT SIGHT   BARREL   FRAME   HAMMER

EJECTOR ROD ASSEMBLY

CYLINDER LOCK SCREW

CYLINDER

TRIGGER PIVOT

EJECTOR SPRING

TRIGGER GUARD   TRIGGER

HAMMER PIVOT

BACKSTRAP

GRIP PANEL SCREW

GRIP PANEL

THE REVOLVER

• Most familiar and usually the preferred sidearm, the revolver provides reliable operation and a stronger construction capable of handling more potent loads than the automatic. In addition, it may be carried loaded without danger of accidental discharge.

The revolver offers a choice of two actions: double and single. In the double-action, each trigger-squeeze cocks the hammer, revolves and positions the cylinder, and fires the gun. In single-actions, the hammer must be cocked manually to position the cylinder. The trigger is then squeezed when the shooter is ready to fire. In all models, cartridges must be loaded manually, one by one. A cylinder usually holds six rounds. To load the double-action, the shooter simply touches the side latch, exposing the cylinder chamber by swinging it out, away from the frame. The cylinder of the single-action does not swing open.

102

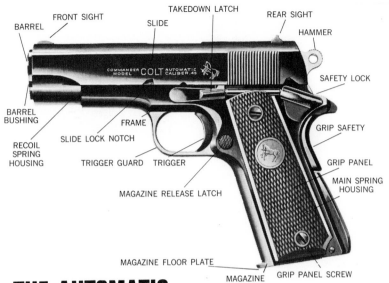

BARREL
FRONT SIGHT
SLIDE
TAKEDOWN LATCH
REAR SIGHT
HAMMER
SAFETY LOCK
BARREL BUSHING
FRAME
GRIP SAFETY
RECOIL SPRING HOUSING
SLIDE LOCK NOTCH
TRIGGER GUARD   TRIGGER
GRIP PANEL
MAIN SPRING HOUSING
MAGAZINE RELEASE LATCH
MAGAZINE FLOOR PLATE
MAGAZINE   GRIP PANEL SCREW

THE AUTOMATIC

• The hard-hitting automatic is a flat, compact arm, easy to carry and conceal, and capable of providing one major advantage: rapidity of fire. It has, however, several drawbacks. The complexity of its design tends to produce uncertain operation. Improper loading or a faulty magazine can cause jamming, and if the gun misfires, it is a two-handed operation to yank the slide back to clear the chamber. These pistols should always be carried with the chamber empty to insure complete safety. All automatics are clip-loaded. The gun's chamber is part of its barrel. For initial firing in single-action models with an external hammer, the slide must be pulled back to cock the gun. This is unnecessary in double-action and hammerless models in which the initial trigger-pull cocks the hammer and fires the gun. Part of the recoil energy moves the parts, ejecting the empty shell and positioning a new cartridge.

CUTAWAY VIEW OF THE DOUBLE-ACTION S & W .38 MILITARY AND POLICE REVOLVER

Each trigger-pull cocks the hammer, positions the cartridge, and fires the gun in double actions. The hammer is raised as sear and hand couple; their release allows the hammer nose to fall, striking the firing pin

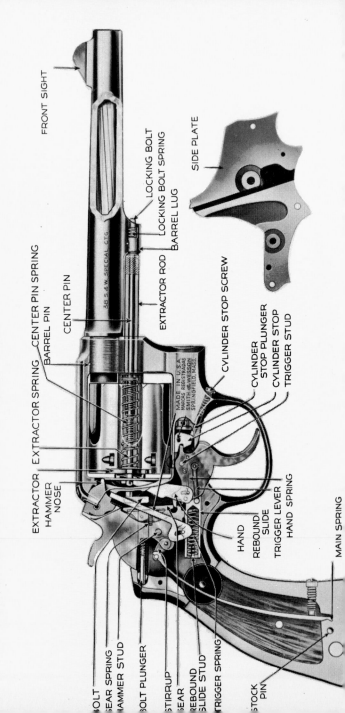

FRONT SIGHT

LOCKING BOLT

LOCKING BOLT SPRING

BARREL LUG

SIDE PLATE

EXTRACTOR SPRING

CENTER PIN SPRING

BARREL PIN

CENTER PIN

EXTRACTOR

HAMMER NOSE

EXTRACTOR ROD

38 S&W SPECIAL CTG.

CYLINDER STOP SCREW

CYLINDER STOP PLUNGER

CYLINDER STOP

TRIGGER STUD

MADE IN U.S.A.
MARCAS REGISTRADAS
SMITH & WESSON
SPRINGFIELD, MASS.

HAND

REBOUND SLIDE

TRIGGER LEVER

HAND SPRING

BOLT

GEAR SPRING

HAMMER STUD

BOLT PLUNGER

STIRRUP

GEAR

REBOUND SLIDE STUD

TRIGGER SPRING

STOCK PIN

MAIN SPRING

CUTAWAY VIEW OF A SINGLE-ACTION RUGER BEARCAT REVOLVER

The hammer of single-action models is cocked manually—simultaneously joining sear and hand and aligning a cartridge. To fire, the shooter squeezes the trigger to release the hammer

RIFLED BARREL

BASE PIN

BASE PIN LATCH NUT

CYLINDER

CYLINDER LATCH PLUNGER

CYLINDER LATCH SPRING

RECOIL PLATE CROSS PIN

CARTRIDGE CHAMBER

FIRING PIN

CYLINDER LATCH

FIRING PIN REBOUND SPRING

HAMMER PIVOT

HAMMER STRUT

TRIGGER SPRING

HAMMER SPRING SEAT

HAMMER SPRING

PP-1

CALIBERS AND AMMUNITION

• There is very little difference between pistol caliber and rifle caliber (see page 24). Pistol barrels are rifled and act upon the bullet in the same manner. Like the rifle, the pistol fires either rim-fire or center-fire cartridges. In .22 caliber, either the hammer or the firing pin, depending on the specific model, strikes the head of the cartridge. All other calibers are center-fire. The firing pin strikes the primer in the middle of the cartridge base. There is a degree of interchangeability in revolver cartridges not found in rifles. The .357 Magnum can also fire the .38 Special, the .44 Magnum also uses the .44 Special, and the .22 Magnum the .22 Special. However, the regular .22 rim-fire cannot handle the Magnums.

Center-fire cartridges for automatics are rimless. This is to permit them to feed easily from the clip magazines. In order to make extraction from the cylinder possible, cartridges designed for revolvers are equipped with rimmed heads.

SMALL-BORE FIELD GUNS

• No other firearm captures the shooter's imagination as readily as the handgun. It is difficult to shoot accurately, of limited use in hunting, and not easy to own because of restrictive legislation, but it is still the firearm that most people think of as "gun" and the one every shooter hopes to possess. In rugged country where the hunter must cross rocky, or wild, terrain and must use both hands to do it, and in areas where cover is good and he can get within 50 yards of his prey, the handgun is a practical hunting arm and an exciting one to use. Handguns are available in what seem endless designs and sizes and in a wide range of calibers, from .22 Short to the .45 Colt. By far the most popular, and the most suitable for small game, is the .22-caliber rim-fire.

SITUATION: Generally the hunter happens upon small game—rabbit, chuck, porcupine—crouching in tall grass, nibbling vegetation, or in the case of squirrel, poised on a low tree limb. Once he has discovered his target, the shooter must be quick and quiet in readying his arm for the kill. All of these animals are extremely wary and swift in flight, and their minute forms permit them to hide easily. If the hunter misjudges his first shot, he probably will not get a second, or the second will be at an elusive and rapidly moving target. For this type of game, the range is short, the fields are open, and the target is big enough to hit without too much difficulty when it is stationary, so hair-splitting accuracy is not necessary. Only a fairly steady hand is demanded. For technique's sake, the shooter should keep a uniform grip and develop a smooth, steady

107

SMALL-BORE FIELD GUNS

trigger-squeeze or he may misdirect the bullet each time he fires. By placing his free hand on the gun butt, the hunter provides just enough support to improve his hold. If he wishes to steady the gun further, he can either assume a sitting position, supporting his elbows with his knees, or he can lie flat on his back, resting his arms on his chest and supporting his head with a stone or log.

SHOOTING REQUIREMENTS: There is no advantage in heavy guns for this type of shooting. The .22-caliber rim-fire, in either single-shot, revolver, or automatic, is recommended. Probably the safest for the average shooter are the single-shot pistol and the revolver, although they handicap firing speed slightly. Both can be carried fully loaded without fear of accidental discharge; each requires a deliberate cocking action to prepare the gun for firing. Even the double-action revolver, which can be cocked and fired simply by pulling the trigger, is usually cocked manually for more accurate shooting. Automatic pistols in .22 caliber

Ruger Single-Six .22 Magnum

Smith & Wesson .22/32 Kit Gun

Above, left, big- and small-bore field guns (top to bottom):
Colt .22 Buntline Scout, Ruger Super Blackhawk .44
Magnum, Smith & Wesson .44 Magnum, Ruger .22 Bearcat

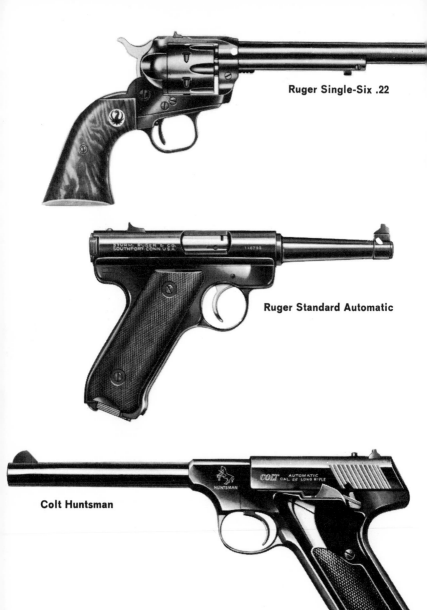

Ruger Single-Six .22

Ruger Standard Automatic

Colt Huntsman

Hi-Standard Double-Nine

SMALL-BORE FIELD GUNS

have internal hammers and can be fired accidentally. They should be carried with the chamber empty. The gun may be readied for action simply by pulling the slide back and allowing it to snap shut. Another drawback of the automatic is its inability to fire any size .22 cartridge other than the Long Rifle (unless especially chambered for the Short). Revolvers take all three cartridge sizes—Short, Long, and Long Rifle. The .22-caliber handgun is usually popular with plinkers since it is inexpensive to fire and lacks the heavy recoil of bigger handguns.

In all cases, when small game is the prey, the gun should be compact enough to carry easily and should be equipped with a medium-length barrel for ease in rapid handling.

Ruger Super Blackhawk .44 Magnum

BIG-BORE FIELD GUNS

• Modern developments in cartridges have made it possible to consider the handgun as a big-game arm. Initial advances toward this end were made more than a decade ago when Major Douglas Wesson, with the aid of western big-game guide Elmer Keith, produced the .357 Magnum cartridge and tested it in a revolver designed especially for the load. The gun was equipped with an 8¾-inch barrel and weighed 47 ounces, the heaviest revolver since the Colt Dragoon cap-and-ball models built during the Civil War period. With his new handgun and cartridge, Wesson was able to kill bull elk, deer, and moose, and after such unusual success wasted no time in placing both cartridge and gun on the market, under the Smith & Wesson label. New big-bore designs not only accommodate these heavy loads, but in the hands of skillful shooters perform almost as effectively as a rifle.

BIG-BORE FIELD GUNS

SITUATION: Handguns in this class are heavy and not easy to carry when on foot, yet they are lighter and less cumbersome than a rifle. In western areas where game is large and the hunter does most of his spotting from the saddle, the big-bore handgun is a convenient sporting arm. It is also handy in emergency situations when a gun must be brought quickly into action. Many guides carry big-bore sidearms for such moments, or to finish a crippled animal, or even to collect "eatin' meat" for camp. These guns are not as limited in range as might be expected, but at long ranges precision is difficult. Yet they produce enough power and operate accurately enough to kill a deer or a black bear at 100 yards, or more, if the bullet strikes the animal directly in the chest cavity. At short ranges they can do justice to just about any hoofed game in the Western Hemisphere. For best performance, a firm grip is essential and developing one requires much practice. The gun should be held so that the backstrap lies in the center of the palm of the shooting hand and the hand is well up on the gun grip. The position should be both firm and comfortable, and it must be one which allows the gunner to squeeze the trigger in a line with barrel, wrist, and forearm, so that the gun recoils straight back. The thumb should never exert pressure, and the grip must be uniform or shots will be thrown to one side or the other, depending upon where the excess pressure exists. The shooter may use his free hand to steady both gun and sight picture.

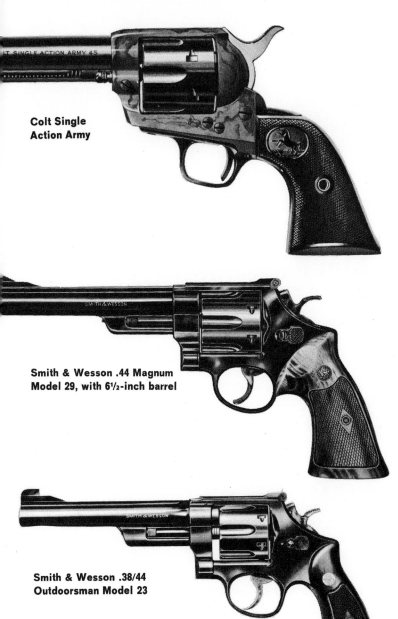

**Colt Single
Action Army**

**Smith & Wesson .44 Magnum
Model 29, with 6½-inch barrel**

**Smith & Wesson .38/44
Outdoorsman Model 23**

115

Ruger Blackhawk .357 Magnum, Presentation Model

BIG-BORE FIELD GUNS

SHOOTING REQUIREMENTS: In the big-bore gun category, the revolver stands alone. No automatic pistol is rugged enough to accommodate these heavy loads. A shooter need only choose between single action and double action. A one-piece, deep-forged frame makes the single-action a slightly superior arm. It is stronger and far less prone to damage. All big-bore models are fitted with hand-filling grips so that the shooter can maintain a firm grasp on his arm. Some are even equipped with adjustable sights; in single action, the Ruger Blackhawk and Colt Frontier; in double action, both Colt and Smith & Wesson models. All three—Colt, Ruger, Smith & Wesson—permit clean, light trigger-pull, insuring greater accuracy at long ranges. Suitable calibers include the modern .357 and .44 Magnum made by Ruger, .45 Colt, and .44 Smith & Wesson Special. Any one of these is powerful enough to fell a deer or similar game at moderate range. The .357 Magnum and the .44 Magnum have an added feature in their ability to fire a low-powered cartridge accurately and effectively. The .357 fires all .38 Special loads—from wadcutters (a bullet with a sharp-edged shoulder that cuts a paper target cleanly, like a conductor's punch) to 200-grain police cartridges. The .44

Shooter reacts to jarring recoil of .44 Magnum

Magnum shoots both .44 Special and .44 Russian. Among big-bore field loads, the .357 Magnum has been the most popular cartridge for over a decade, but it is slowly losing its prominence to the newer, more powerful .44 Magnum, which shoots a 240-grain bullet at 1560 fps muzzle velocity. Both are effective for big-game shooting.

A handloader can improve any of these cartridges by composing more powerful loads for his personal use. Factory loads in these calibers are deliberately "loaded-down" for safety purposes.

117

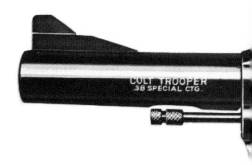

POLICE AND DEFENSE GUNS

• The law officer has more at stake than any other shooter when choosing a suitable handgun. For him, the gun is a defensive arm and must be capable of doing the job unfailingly. The choices available to him are wide, ranging from little "hideout" guns used by plainclothesmen to powerful Magnums used by highway patrolmen.

SITUATION: Almost every phase of police work places a different demand on the design of the handgun. All must be durable to withstand rough and excessive handling. Some must be powerful enough to penetrate the steel of fleeing autos. Detectives and FBI agents need a gun that is easily concealed in shoulder or belt holsters, a gun that will not catch on clothing when snapped swiftly into use. A patrolman walking the beat is not so limited, but his sidearm should be neither too heavy nor too bulky to be carried comfortably in a belt holster for several hours a

Colt Trooper .38 Special

Smith & Wesson 9mm Model 39

Smith & Wesson Highway Patrolman

POLICE AND DEFENSE GUNS

day. Since he is primarily concerned with obtaining power and accuracy for long-range shooting, a long-barreled gun is generally preferable. The same arm would not be suitable for officers assigned to patrol cars. Although these men also need an arm that supplies sufficient power to halt an escaping culprit at long range, the long barrel is too likely to catch on car seats and inhibit an officer's rapid movement in and out of vehicles.

SHOOTING REQUIREMENTS: In spite of the automatic pistol's compact qualities and facility of concealment, the more certain operation of the revolver

Two hands, available rest, aid accuracy

is preferred in police work. When time is short, the possibility of gun-jam because of improper loading or a faulty magazine or cartridge is too great. The official—and most popular—revolver among lawmen in metropolitan areas is chambered for the .38 Special cartridge, a powerful, accurate load. A patrolman on foot usually carries a .38 revolver equipped with a five- or six-inch barrel. At long ranges, the larger sighting radius the long barrel provides increases his chances for accuracy. The same arm with a four-inch barrel is used by mobile units. The shorter barrel fits snugly into a belt holster, is comfortable to wear while

121

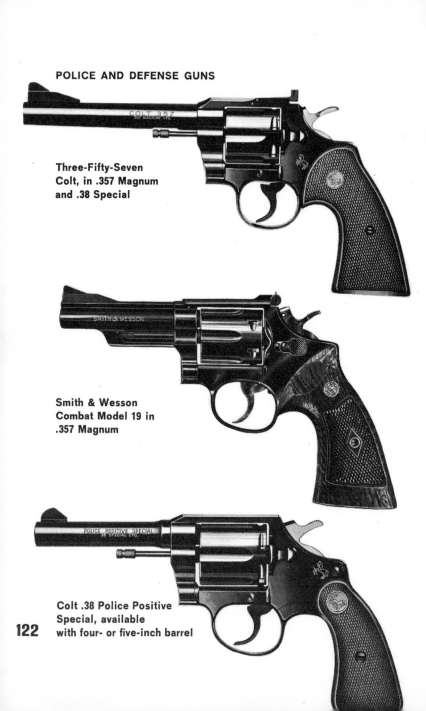

POLICE AND DEFENSE GUNS

Three-Fifty-Seven Colt, in .357 Magnum and .38 Special

Smith & Wesson Combat Model 19 in .357 Magnum

Colt .38 Police Positive Special, available with four- or five-inch barrel

Smith & Wesson .38/44
Heavy Duty Model 20, fires
six shots, has fixed sights

Smith & Wesson
1950 Army Model 22
in .45 caliber

Smith & Wesson .38 Military
and Police Model 10,
with square butt, short action

POLICE AND DEFENSE GUNS

driving, and allows lawmen to move in and out of autos freely. Detectives prefer a snub-nosed model with two-inch barrel because it is easily concealed. It imposes a handicap in running gun fights where ranges exceed 25 yards, but in tight spots, where action must be quick, it performs perfectly. Highway patrolmen, state troopers, sheriffs in rural areas—those who may be in-

volved in taking a criminal at long range or in high-

way chases require more power than the .38 provides.
For years, the Colt .45 was their standard arm, but the
.357 Magnum is gradually replacing it. Designed with
a 3½-inch barrel—about as short a barrel as is practical for a gun of this power and size—the .357 Magnum
is also carried by FBI agents. It provides power, yet
is neither too large nor too bulky to be neatly concealed in a belt holster.

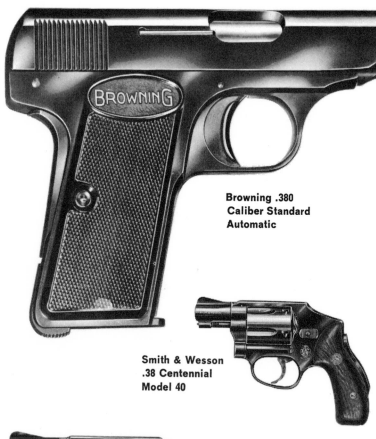

Browning .380
Caliber Standard
Automatic

Smith & Wesson
.38 Centennial
Model 40

Smith & Wesson
.38 Chiefs Special
Model 36

**Colt's Detective
Special
in .38 Special**

**Colt Government
Model .45
caliber automatic**

127

THE TARGET GUN
PART 5

SMALL-BORE RIFLES

• For the past 150 years or so, Americans have been known for their skill with a rifle, and target shooting in its many forms has been an extremely popular sport. Skilled riflemen ranked in status and popularity with today's home-run hitters. Although these pioneer shooters achieved remarkable scores with their early arms, today's demand for even greater accuracy has increased the need for highly specialized rifles and the competence of contemporary riflemen. Youngsters are now encouraged through their schools and organizations such as the National Rifle Association and the Boy Scouts to become familiar with firearms and develop accuracy in shooting.

There are four certified positions for target shooting: prone (for beginners; also the easiest and highest scoring), sitting, kneeling, and standing (the most difficult). The shooter generally fires at a standard target from prescribed distances. This is an intensely competitive sport among youngsters and adult rifle-

Winchester Model 52D
without sights

men alike throughout the country.

Target arms differ appreciably from sporting arms in that handling ease, weight, and size are not of prime importance. Pinpoint accuracy is the goal and the rifle that achieves it is the rifle to use, even though it may be heavy and clumsy by the hunter's standards.

With few exceptions, the .22 is the standard target rifle. Loaded with .22-caliber match ammunition, this arm will give minute-of-angle accuracy up to 100 yards. ("Minute-of-angle" is calculated at one inch for a range of 100 yards. Thus, the .22 rim-fire will, ideally, put all of its bullets into a 1-inch area at 100 yards, something difficult to achieve with high-powered hunting rifles.) The report with this caliber is low and the recoil almost non-existent.

As speed of fire is not an important consideraton in small-bore target shooting, the rugged but slow bolt-action dominates the choice of target arms. Some shooters prefer to load each cartridge singly to avoid **131**

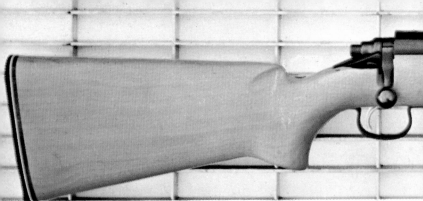

Remington Model 40X Rangemaster

SMALL-BORE RIFLES

the risk of damaging the bullet when it is fed through the magazine.

RECOMMENDED GUNS: Tops among match rifles are the single-shot bolt-action Remington Model 40X and the Winchester Model 52, which comes with a single-shot adapter. Other rifles, more modestly priced than

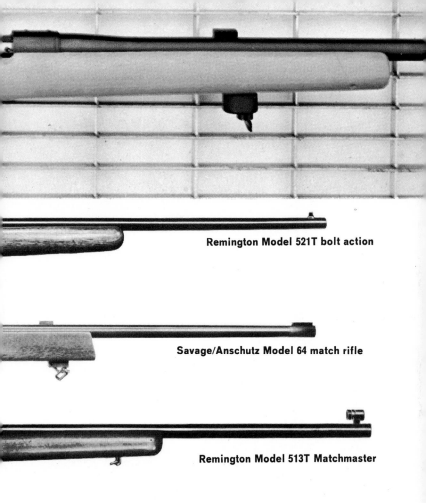

Remington Model 521T bolt action

Savage/Anschutz Model 64 match rifle

Remington Model 513T Matchmaster

these excellent models, are the Mossberg 144LS, and lighter-weight Remington Model 513T and Winchester Model 52 with standard-weight barrel. When fitted with aperture (peep) sights, they perform very well in all but the highest match competition and will help the beginner to develop considerable skill on the range. **133**

SMALL-BORE RIFLES

These rifles are equipped with delicate trigger-pull adjustments to assure the finest let-off possible, and every effort is made to bring out all of the accuracy inherent in the .22 Long Rifle cartridge. However, a serious target shooter who is satisfied with nothing less than maximum scoring, commonly called "possibles," must have the best rifle available. This means the top-grade Winchester or Remington. These rifles will give fine performances in both prone and four-position match shooting. However, most serious riflemen usually alter the stock to make it conform to their own individual style of shooting.

Mossberg Model 144LS (top),
and Mossberg Model 346B.
Youths (below) practice on range

BIG-BORE RIFLES

• Except for the military-match competitors, few target shooters have the opportunity to compete in long-range center-fire matches—which means shooting a center-fire rifle at ranges up to and including 1,000 yards. This is an expensive sport for the civilian because of high ammunition costs, and because the club ranges offering this type of shooting are limited.

RECOMMENDED GUNS: Many center-fire competitors use the National Match Springfield rifle, which can be obtained through the Director of Civilian Marksmanship, and the NRA at 1600 Rhode Island Avenue, N.W., Washington, D.C. Among private gunmakers, only Winchester and Remington offer top-grade arms for this kind of shooting. Winchester's Model 70 .300 H. & H. Magnum is best; also good are the Model 70 Target Rifle in .30-06 and Remington 40XB in long-range match calibers. **135**

Remington International Match

FREE RIFLES AND PISTOLS

• The most exacting form of rifle shooting is the free rifle match. The shooter must fire over a 300-meter (327-yard) range from prone, kneeling, and offhand (standing) positions at a target whose 10-ring (the bull's-eye) has a diameter of less than four inches. Only iron sights may be used. Until recently, no free rifles were manufactured in this country and Americans were forced to use foreign makes for this difficult competition. However, sparked by the 1960 Olympics, both Winchester and Remington have developed specialized .30-caliber center-fire free rifles.

High on the list of competitive free rifles is the Savage/Anschutz—made in several match calibers—with which several Olympic medals have been won recently. Unfortunately, there is no American-made pistol for International Free Pistol competition.

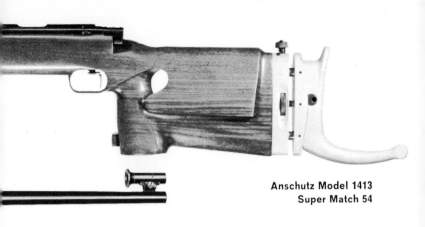

Anschutz Model 1413
Super Match 54

Winchester's free rifle. Spotting scope shows location of hit

Remington Model 1100 automatic

Savage Model 30 pump-action shotgun

SKEET SHOOTING

• Skeet received its name in a contest held in 1925. The word is Scandinavian and—appropriately—means "shoot." Skeet is a fast, short-range game with a moving clay target, and is designed to simulate small upland-game hunting. The field is laid out in an arc, with seven shooting stations at equal distances along its perimeter and two traps, one at each end of the arc. An eighth station lies at midpoint on a line between the traps. Birds are thrown in two flight paths that cross five yards in front of Station 8. Shooting from each station, the gunner gets many angles, both incoming and outgoing, including doubles. The shooter may have his gun at the ready and knows the precise flight of the bird. The target is broken at an average of 22 yards.

The most effective skeet guns are the short-barreled, open-bored guns similar to those used in upland hunting. Any gauge is permitted, but the 12, with its powerful load, is still the most advantageous. In order to maintain competitive equality, shooters using the small gauges—20 to .410—compete among themselves.

Instructor studies performance of novice shotgunner

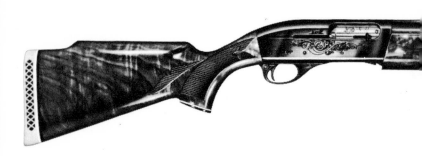

Browning Superposed 20 gauge

Remington Model 11-48 SA

Savage Model 30 featherweight

Winchester Model 1200 Skeet

Remington Model 1100TB Automatic Trap Gun

TRAPSHOOTING

• Trap is the long-range, clay-target game that approximates shooting at waterfowl and large upland game. The trap is thrown from a single trap house located in front of the shooting posts. In singles shooting, the target is thrown at varied angles of which the shooter is not forewarned. In doubles, the flight paths are fixed. In both cases the birds always move away from the shooter. The shooter stands at a minimum of 16 yards behind the trap house and the targets fly from 48 to 52 yards. The target is the same clay bird used in skeet shooting, but, unlike skeet, the gunner is permitted to take aim—usually over the trap house—before calling for his bird. Hits occur at about 35 yards.

The trap gun is built especially for this sport and is seldom used for anything else. A 12-gauge gun with a minimum barrel length of 30 inches is the best choice.

Browning Superposed 12 gauge

Remington Model 870 TX

Winchester Model 1400 Trap Gun

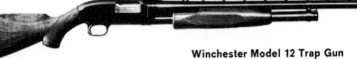

Winchester Model 12 Trap Gun

Clay bird in hand trap is released when swung

HAND-TRAP AND UTILITY GUNS

• Hand-trapping is an uncomplicated sport that requires only enough space, a trap and someone to operate it, and a gun. The hand trap is a small lightweight (usually under a pound) device with a spring mechanism. It holds the clay bird and releases it when swung manually. Hand-trapping can go further than skeet in exploiting every possible angle of fire for field shooting practice. There is no fixed range, but a minimum of 300 yards in front of the shooter is necessary as a safety precaution.

144   Hand-trapping can be practiced with any kind of

Hand-trapping is an eye-sharpener for field gunners

Marlin Model 55, 12 gauge, adjustable choke

shotgun—the low-priced single shots and bolt actions known as utility guns, as well as guns designed for specific hunting or target work. As in skeet shooting, the bigger the gun's gauge, the cleaner the break. But because of its light weight and low recoil, the little .410 is a favorite. The shooter must be right on target, however, to compensate for the small shot pattern. A good .410 in the utility class is the Savage over/under rifle and shotgun made with .410 gauge combined with .22 or .22 Magnum. Also fine, economical arms for general shotgunning are bolt-action repeaters.

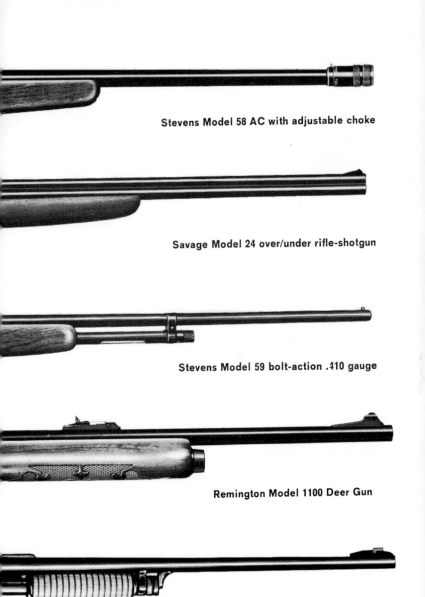

Stevens Model 58 AC with adjustable choke

Savage Model 24 over/under rifle-shotgun

Stevens Model 59 bolt-action .410 gauge

Remington Model 1100 Deer Gun

Ithaca Model 37 Deerslayer Rifled-Slug Special

TARGET HANDGUNS

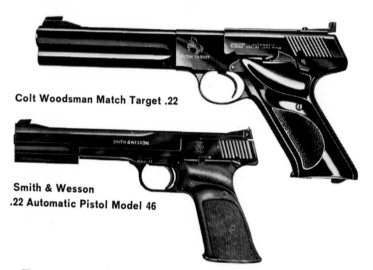

Colt Woodsman Match Target .22

Smith & Wesson
.22 Automatic Pistol Model 46

• Target-pistol shooting is an extremely exacting sport in which the shooter's form and actions must be standardized as much as possible. He must shoot the same way each time. The only way to master this is through practice and by using the most accurate pistol obtainable. The point of aim, sight picture, and grip must be constant. Grip is most important in big-bore events because of the recoil of the big-caliber pistols. There is a tendency for the gun to shift in the hand after each shot. This changes the sight picture and makes it impossible to maintain maximum accuracy. The novice frequently must fight against uneven trigger-pull. Instead of simply pulling back on the trigger, he pulls back and to the right. Both firmness of grip and an even pull are things that can only be achieved through conscientious, unremitting practice.

Ruger Mark I .22-caliber automatic

Smith & Wesson K-38 Model 14

TARGET HANDGUNS

The refinements that contribute to accuracy in a target handgun include sufficient weight for steady holding in stiff breezes, a clean, light trigger-pull, non-slip trigger, ample barrel length for a long sight radius, sights that adjust with ease and accuracy, and a comfortable, hand-filling grip. All target handguns fulfill these requirements, but to varying degrees.

In small-bore (.22 rim-fire) target shooting, the automatic pistol is the popular favorite, particularly in timed-fire and rapid-fire matches. Timed fire is 20 seconds for five shots; rapid fire, 10 seconds for five. The self-loading, self-cocking features of this action en-

Colt Python .357 Magnum

S & W .22 Automatic Pistol Model 41

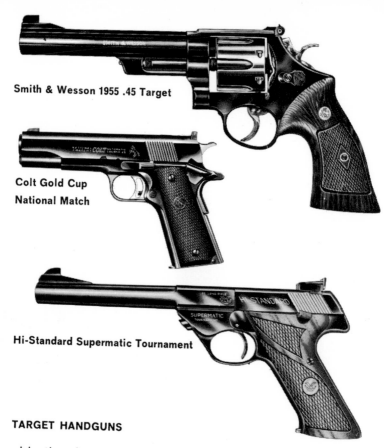

Smith & Wesson 1955 .45 Target

**Colt Gold Cup
National Match**

Hi-Standard Supermatic Tournament

TARGET HANDGUNS

able the shooter to concentrate on the target. Even in slow-fire competition, the small-bore automatic is inherently more accurate than the revolver.

In most big-bore matches, the reverse is true and the revolver is essential. It is difficult to develop a fine trigger-pull in an automatic because of the nature of the action. Virtually the only qualifying center-fire autoloader in a standard arm is the Colt .45 National Match. However, experts have converted the Colt Government Model .45 to handle the .38 Special cartridge and, in the process, have made the entire action more accu-

Hi-Standard Supermatic Trophy Presentation Model .22 automatic

rate. This is effective, but expensive, as it demands the finest gunsmithing.

High-grade revolvers in the Colt and Smith & Wesson lines perform with amazing accuracy and facility in the hands of a skilled target shooter. However, they are somewhat slower than autos in the fast-firing matches. The .38 Special and the .44 Special are the preferred calibers in revolvers, both of which can be fired in the big .357 and .44 Magnums. While Magnum cartridges are not used for target shooting, these big-caliber revolvers make fine, steady-holding target guns.

153

GUN CARE AND MAINTENANCE

Fine steel wool, followed by cleaning patch, removes leading

• Good gun care these days means little more than protecting the external metal surface from rust. Actually, a rifle fired with modern ammunition is better left uncleaned if it is not going to be idle too long under humid conditions. The thin film of powder and the powder residue left after firing are usually good protection against rust.

EQUIPMENT: Tools for gun care are simple: 3/0 steel wool for rust removal; cleaning patches and a stiff, jointed cleaning rod with a swivel tip for each bore

To guard against moisture, use paste wax, then polish it off

size or gauge; solvent (Winchester Solvent, Hoppe's #9, or acetone); a silicone-impregnated cloth (or oil and a wiping rag); a tube of gun grease, and a can of paste wax meet the needs of general maintenance.

SHOTGUNS: The thin-walled barrel of a shotgun is especially susceptible to dents. If dents occur, don't attempt to shoot them out. Take the gun to a gunsmith who has the proper expanding "dent-raiser" for repair. If the muzzle end of a rifle or shotgun has been jammed into snow, clay, or mud, check after unloading for ob-

155

structions and remove them with a pocketknife or a stick. Don't try to shoot such a plug out of the barrel.

After about a hundred shells have been fired, new shotguns often show streaks of lead in the bore—just in front of the chamber or near the muzzle. This indicates some roughness in the bore, but that will smooth out with continued shooting. Remove the streaks by wrapping a wad of the fine steel wool around the cleaning patch on the shotgun rod and scrubbing out the bore thoroughly.

HANDGUNS: The chambers and barrel of a handgun can be cleaned easily with a bristle brush soaked with powder solvent. Wipe the bore with dry patches and oil it lightly if it is to be inactive for a time. Go over the outside parts with the silicone cloth, or apply light oil. Use heavier gun grease in very humid areas.

RIFLES: To clean the bore, run a patch wet with solvent through it. Follow with a dry patch. Examine the bore for lumps—rust, metal or lead fouling. If they appear, wrap steel wool around a patch and polish them out. If the rifle is to be used again soon, oil the bore lightly. Coat it with gun grease if it is to be stored for a long period.

Self-loading .22 rim-fire rifles and automatic pistols require extra breech care because of powder residue. Swab the breech with powder solvent. If much grease is present, use alcohol or carbon tetrachloride.

Oil should not be squirted at random into the action of any gun. It tends to pick up additional abrasive dust and can cause problems. If the gun is to be used at temperatures near zero, flush it clean with carbon tetrachloride or gasoline, allow it to dry, then lubricate **156** with powdered graphite.

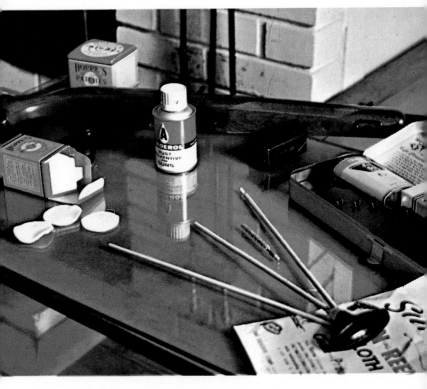

Basic equipment for gun care includes: Gun oil, powder solvent, and patches (in box, right); jointed aluminum cleaning rod; jet-spray rust preventative; silicone-impregnated cloth

If a gun must be exposed to wet weather, go over it beforehand with a paste wax, then polish it off. Should the gun get soaked, either by heavy rain or immersion, tie it, muzzle down, to the back of a chair and place it near a warm radiator or open oven to dry. Polish it with a dry cloth, then wipe with the silicone cloth or oily rag.

INDEX OF GUNS Numbers in **bold face** refer to illustrations.